S0-AZM-419

Sex at Work

Sex at Work

A Survival Guide

Judi James

The Industrial Society

First published in 1998 by 658.3145
The Industrial Society $J 279$
Robert Hyde House
48 Bryanston Square
London W1H 7LN
Telephone: 0171 479 2000

Copyright Judi James 1998
Typographical arrangement copyright The Industrial Society 1998

ISBN 1 85835 570 2

Stylus Publishing Inc
22883 Quicksilver Drive
Sterling
VA 20166-2012
USA

British Library Cataloguing-in-Publication Data.
A catalogue record for this publication is available from the
British Library.

All rights reserved. No part of this publication may be reproduced,
stored in a retrieval system or transmitted, in any form or by any means,
electronic, mechanical, photocopying, recording and/or otherwise
without the prior written permission of the publishers. This publication
may not be lent, resold, hired out or otherwise disposed of by way of
trade in any form, binding or cover other than that in which it is
published, without the prior consent of the publishers.

Typeset by: The Midlands Book Typesetting Co.
Printed by: Lavenham Press
Cover design: Sign
Cover photo: Getty Images

The Industrial Society is a Registered Charity No. 290003

Contents

Sex at Work

Sex at work is one of life's great inevitables. The office affair has been – and always will be – a regular feature of business culture, along with all the little core industries that thrive on it, like gossip, speculation and rumour-spreading.

Sex has been used to launch some careers – via the casting couch – but it has also been known to scupper them too. In terms of job security it is always a risky option.

During the recent wave of political correctness sex became banned at work along with smoking, although (unlike smoking) no rooms were put aside in offices for people who still wanted to indulge! Sexual harassment evolved from being a boss's perk into a legal minefield, with reported cases increasing steadily as both male and female staff realised that bullying and victimisation weren't the only options.

So how does the current climate of sex in the workplace look? A recent survey of office workers showed that at least 40 per cent of them claimed to have had a romance or an affair with a colleague, so business is obviously still booming. Companies are becoming increasingly aware of their duties in protecting harassed employees, although the situation is far from perfect. At one end of the scale the age-old problems still exist. Staff are harassed and badly so. At the other end of the scale nervous, politically aware managers are barricading themselves in their offices away from the opposite sex, fearful that one glance in the wrong direction may lead to a court case. In the meantime there are mutually attracted people meeting partners at work and then having to navigate through all the perils of an ongoing, desk-bound relationship.

This book, then, is a guide to all aspects of sex in the workplace.

First, some vital ground rules:

1. This book does not intend to finger-wag or take a high moral tone.
2. It will not create rules but will provoke thought and offer positive strategies.
3. It accepts that men can be sexually harassed as well as women.
4. This book is aimed at all sexual preferences apart from the wildly obscure or off-the-wall.
5. It is vital reading for any man or woman for whom sex in the workplace is a potential, viable, pursued, avoided or even ongoing option.
6. It will work under the premise that:

- Sex is great.
- Sex can introduce a little intrigue into an otherwise boring day.
- Bromide should only be introduced into the coffee machine under extreme circumstances!

However (and there had to be a 'but', didn't there?), it should also be remembered that:

1. Sex + Business = Trouble.
2. Sex is an emotional mental state while business requires analytical decision-making.
3. Sex is frequently a career-limiting manoeuvre.
   (These days 'sleeping your way to the top' tends to refer to executive catnaps following large liquid lunches.) The only safe sex at work is no sex.

Or, to put it another way, it can – and often does – all end in tears. Embarrassment, confrontation, decruitment (and any other euphemisms for getting fired), being taken to court: any and all of these can occur when lust supplants logic.

Here is a dip-in guide, then, providing advice on damage-avoidance as well as damage-limitation. Use it as the voice of reason before, during and even after things seem to be getting out of hand.

CHAPTER 1

Only a Bit of a Laugh

> If a woman dresses attractively I assume she wants to be
> looked at. Why would she do it otherwise? If she didn't
> want me looking she would wear an old cardigan and
> slacks, wouldn't she?
>
> *Partner in a solicitors' practice*

> I can't see anything wrong with having a joke. The
> women here take the mickey out of the young lads all
> the time. They know we don't mean it.
>
> *Office manager*

When tiptoeing through the minefield that is sexual harassment in
modern business a key component has to be considered at all times:
perception.

Perception

Pushing legal guidelines to one side for a moment (although they will
be touched on in Chapter 11), it is important to remember that we all
view the world through a different set of eyes. You have your own
perceptions of what is inappropriate or intolerable behaviour, but even
those standards may be flexible.

For instance, you may well be more tolerant towards people you like than to those you can't stand. Or you might laugh long and loud at a blue joke told by a comedian you find funny but take a priggish U-turn if the geek at the next desk uses the same kind of language.

What is considered right or wrong behaviour is largely a matter of personal perception. It is possible to offer guidelines for top-of-the-range misdemeanours, but who can tell someone they are wrong if they find very minor transgressions a virtual hanging offence?

The whole area of inappropriate behaviour is murky. For instance, there would surely be a unanimous show of hands if I asked whether unapproved groping was inappropriate behaviour. But what if I asked whether compliments about personal appearance should be out of bounds at work? And if you shook your head till the dandruff flew over that one, think: surely it depends on what particular aspect of the appearance is being complimented?

We are in the era of PPC (Post-Political Correctness), which in turn was a backlash to the macho Eighties, which followed the heavy feminism of the Seventies, which came in the wake of the permissive Sixties ... and so on.

Wherever the tidemarks of law and conventional boundaries settle, though, you must always be flexible in a downward direction. None of us is 'right' in our perceptions. We only hold a viewpoint, but that view is our own standard and should be respected by others.

Your Angle on Life

How did you learn your own perceptions of life and what is right and what is wrong? How did you discover the correct rules of sexual etiquette? (Or maybe you're still trying to find out.) Did anyone sit you down and tell you what you should and shouldn't do? And if so, in how much detail?

Most of the stuff we learn about appropriate behaviour comes from any or all of the following:

● Parents.
● Teachers.
(Although their training focuses heavily on the reproductive system

of rabbits, rather than how to succeed on a Saturday night, much to the disappointment of generations of gangly youths hoping that school would finally teach them something they *wanted* to know.)
- Other kids (with the sexual etiquette skills of your average baboon).
- Church.
- Television.
- Reading matter (*Janet and John Go on a Hot Date*).
- Our so-called superiors, i.e. Royalty, peers of the realm, politicians, etc. (Heaven help us.)
- Other heroes, i.e. sports-people, celebrities, etc. (Ditto.)

Things look murkier by the minute.

However it was pitched, then, your upbringing had a lot to do with shaping your current views of what is right and what is wrong. Well, we all had a different upbringing. None of us is the same. We all emerge from a different set of experiences. That's what makes us so fascinating. No two people think in exactly the same way, not even identical twins. We see everything in this life through different eyeballs and that's fine, as long as we respect other viewpoints. If we don't we are bigots. Bigots make assumptions about other people. They think they are right, but then again, so do we all (about most things, anyway). What makes the bigot so different is that his or her 'rightness' is inflexible and non-negotiable.

Very rarely are opinions 'right' or 'wrong'. Usually they are just 'different': we all hold our own views. Expecting others automatically to fall in with those views is clearly impractical.

Take some of the most recent cases of sexual harassment to have hit the headlines. Most of them are the subject of heated debate around dinner tables throughout the country. Was the woman right in claiming sexual harassment over a birthday strippergram? Did a boss have the right to recommend a high-flyer should wait before starting a family? Should sending those suggestive e-mails constitute a sacking offence?

Everyone holds their own opinion and most are offered happily and confidently, without a full grasp of the facts of the story, which is why the law is brought in to make official judgement. But how many situations would not have been converted into crises if the people involved had been more attuned to others' feelings and views in the first place?

Fail-safe

In business we have a behavioural yardstick to turn to whenever we are in doubt about the correctness of our sexual judgement: professionalism.

There is no need to bring sex into the work environment: we each have a social life where things can be a lot less complicated. So the motto should be:

If in doubt, leave it out.

Sounds dull, doesn't it?

How else to fill those yawning hours between nine and five if gossip, flirting, risqué jokes and speculation about affairs are all wiped off the menu? Well, I suppose you could always try work.

'Pulling off-piste' is a lot less dangerous than the office liaison because sexual behaviour at work comes with its own hidden agenda. It is a complex business. There is always more at stake than a quick fling. Relationships with colleagues are difficult enough to maintain without an affair pitching the whole thing out of kilter. Like the butterfly flapping its wings and sparking a tidal wave on the other side of the planet, sex at work has ramifications that will normally affect more than just the couple involved. Favouritism, nepotism and breaches of confidentiality are just three of the charges that can be levelled against the 'happy' couple, and that's just if the whole affair is well balanced and avoids charges of sexual harassment or adultery.

Just be careful, that's all:

1. Understand that what *you* consider 'jokey' behaviour may be offensive to someone else.
2. Never assume.
3. Never continue an approach after someone has asked you not to, or has said 'no'. Always take people at their word.
4. Remember that what *you* consider to be appropriate behaviour may be entirely inappropriate to someone else. Respect their opinions, don't argue with them or mock them.

CHAPTER 2

Mixing Business with Pleasure

> I admit that Karen and I met at work. I think that's
> where most couples do meet. Sometimes there's very
> little alternative when you're working with someone
> until late every evening.
>
> *Chief executive officer*

What is it about the workplace that seems to make sexual shenanigans so unavoidable? Why is business such a powerful aphrodisiac? Well, the answer may be contained in some or all of the following:

A Confined Space

Put any number of people of the opposite, or even the same, sex in a room together for hours at a time and the odds are that hormones will start buzzing and testosterone flowing before long.

Hours to Spend

The British have the longest working hours in Europe, which means more time spent away from conventional partners.

Power Stations

Power is supposed to turn people on. I say 'supposed' because most powerful women surveyed claimed men did not seem as turned on by a powerful woman as women did by a powerful man. (Discuss.)

Whether or not it attracts other people, power can certainly act as an aphrodisiac for the powerful person themselves. Successful people are frequently confident people and confidence is a vital component in the 'I fancy myself and so should you' stakes.

A Diversion

Office work can be boring and sexual *frisson* can relieve the boredom. This is a very serious point. When you get bored your levels of discrimination tend to drop. Think holiday romance and then quadruple the effect. Did you ever see that holiday passion-pants back in Blighty? Bear this in mind when taking a potential office partner into the real world. Friends sometimes think you have cracked when they meet this corporate sex god out of context. You find yourself explaining that this individual is in fact an omnipotent line-manager while all your mates see is a pasty-faced elderly character with a penchant for handknits. This can be dangerous. Real, mind-numbing boredom may lead you into fantasising about people you would normally not contemplate donating pillow-space to. Love is supposed to be blind but office romances are often deaf and dumb too.

Dressed to Thrill?

People at work usually dress smarter than they do at home, therefore appearing marginally more attractive in a suit than they do in their baggy tracksuit bottoms and geriatric bedroom slippers.

Hyped-up and Raring to Go

They may also be more alert and a lot more 'gung-ho' at work than they are at home, where that business buccaneer with a 'can do' attitude tends to turn into an overtired couch potato with barely enough energy to kiss the kids goodnight.

Shared Goals

Working as a team and sharing aims, daily ambitions and loyal relationships can form strong interpersonal bonds, as anyone in the armed forces will tell you. It is easy for all that bonding in the office to go a step too far.

Dating Agency

For those past the age of clubbing and wine bars it can be difficult – if not impossible – to find suitable places to meet a partner (unless you include supermarkets and the ghastly 'arranged date' dinner parties).

Work, then, may seem like the only alternative. Don't forget, though, that unlike the supermarket and dinner party, if the whole thing turns unpleasant, and even hostile, you may well be forced to meet up with that person again each and every working weekday.

Nature's Bromide

Nature has, however, to a certain extent, designed its own natural remedies to all these passion-enhancers, like:

Sad-cladding

The business suit. Smart it may be, but revealing it ain't. Head and hands are the only flesh visible.

Stress

The most effective way of stopping all those hormones and testosterone in their tracks. Stress levels in business are high and currently rising. Good stress-surfing brings about the old adrenalin rush that can engender frisky behaviour, but negative stress can make you too tired and anxious even to notice the sex of the person working next to you, let alone fancy them.

Downsizing

Which means added workloads which equals 'Too busy to even think about it'.

Bad Habits

Unattractive office behaviour like knuckle-cracking, foot tapping, slurping coffee too loudly, whistling, loud yawning or noisy eating are all common practices in open-plan offices and can constitute a great turn-off.

Mating Call

So, what are the advantages and disadvantages of meeting a mate in the workplace?

It has been estimated that up to 50 per cent of us meet our future partners through or at work, which makes it a significant venue for budding romance.

There are obvious plus points to meeting your partner at work:

1. You know you will have at least one thing in common, as well as an informed ear to bounce all your troubles off when you get home in the evening.
2. You will probably have had the opportunity to study this person quite closely before starting to date them. Work is a way of test-driving a potential partner (i.e. getting to know them) before taking the plunge and asking them out. Better still, you'll be seeing them during the day, rather than just propping up a bar with them in the evening. This system obviously has its advantages over night-time pick-ups in a darkened club, holiday romances that are notoriously short-lived, or blind dates arranged by friends.
3. The convenience factor. Work together during the day, pop out for a quick drink after work, Bob's your uncle. High-powered city workers of the Nineties are accustomed to using the office as a complete life-support system. Food is brought in to them. Drinks are on tap. Everything is on order, from stress-busting massage at the desk to on-site counselling, so why not pick a mate there too?

However, before you go hopping off into the sunset with Quentin/ Denise from Accounts, you should carefully take the downside of the situation into consideration.

Office Gossip

Do you want to be the prime target of office gossip? Do you think your career will be enhanced if you are? Office gossip is nearly as old as sex itself. It's fun, it's fascinating and – thanks to the introduction of e-mail – details of your jolly little affair can be broadcast through the entire building in the blink of an eye.

Never labour under the illusion that you can keep the whole thing under wraps. Rest assured that the gossips will have had you sussed from that first smouldering glance across the fax machine. People at a surprisingly high level in companies enjoy a bit of gossip: one manager used to call his secretary into his office once a week for a regular de-briefing, asking her what the latest gossip was. He didn't want to be seen to be indulging himself, so he'd send her out on a trawl on his behalf.

Where boredom kicks in so does the hunt for a bit of intrigue to spice up the coffee break. For some workers the office is just like a daily dose of their favourite soap and if no plot exists they'll happily invent one.

Never think you have to be indulging in a bit of hanky-panky to be accused of it. In some large companies the level of gossip is so high that people get disappointed if they're not the subject of it at some time.

Staying Silent

I would say that you should never indulge in gossip yourself. I *should* say that it can be harmful and malicious, which it can. I would love to reassure you that I never indulge myself, that it's not funny and it's definitely not clever. Unfortunately you need a will of iron not to be guilty of gossiping now and again.

Not muck-spreading yourself is relatively easy. You know that's wrong and being professional means being discreet. My own lips would stay sealed even if I found out a colleague was providing sado-masochistic services to the entire boardroom. But refusing to *listen* when that information passed my shell-likes? Doesn't information equal power?

Remember how much gossip is based on fiction, though. Think how easily it can wreck someone's personal life. Let's call this the Othello Factor. When in doubt, remember what rumour-spreading led to there.

Then you have your own image to think of. Being seen to indulge in gossip is very uncool and a bad career move if you're edging towards promotion. Being indiscreet about colleagues will imply to a manager that you're indiscreet about the company too. Gossiping may make you instantly popular but anyone who listens will work out sooner or later that you'll be talking about them too, when their back is turned. This could soon lead to a 'negative-friend situation'.

If you're really hooked then get yourself a job on a Sunday tabloid instead. Or at least read the things and then confine your work gossip to subjects like celebrities or politicians. Surely there's enough mileage for you there?

So none of that tittle-tattle, then. Be discreet. Tell people you're not interested if they come round gossiping to you. This rarely stops them, by the way. The true gossip will only see this as a challenge to their powers. If you refuse to listen they will go out of their way to tempt you with such intriguing titbits you'd need to be a saint not to ask to hear more.

I find it difficult not to listen to every bit of information that crosses my path in the workplace. Gossip, then, is part of that information. What I feel is important is that I don't encourage it, spread it or believe it. (Until I see the evidence myself, that is.) And yes, you would be right to point out that listening is, in itself, passive encouragement.

Smoking Them Out

The workplace gossip is easy to unearth by the simple and well-tried act of passing disinformation. Make something up that is harmless but juicy. Tell a colleague 'in strictest confidence' and see how long it takes to get back to you. The most harmful gossips should be dealt with by management before they undermine the entire workforce. Like Iago, they are quite capable of spreading lies just to further their own careers or standing.

Office Politics – Falling Foul of the System

Another pitfall to keep in mind before you launch off on your own little trail of romantic ecstasy is office politics.

Most companies work on a fragile but vital network of relationships, pecking orders and hierarchies. Inside this complex network are trouble spots, ranging from quick spats to major power struggles. The late Nineties may be the era of the 'new niceness' at work, with colleagues bonding and team-building, with support groups of counsellors and psychologists ensuring everyone gets along just fine, but let's for one minute suppose that we are still all human and that all this niceness will still be prone to an attack of the dangerous hotspots.

Now, normal business relationships tend to rub along, albeit with the normal problems. Sex, however, can cause a major internal imbalance. Even if the whole thing is merrily reciprocated and happily out in the open, colleagues may still feel uneasy. What was two will suddenly become one. This may not just unsettle your colleagues, it may well be frowned on by the company itself.

Pillow Talk

Whether you like it or not, your blissful affair may well have far-reaching effects. Depending on the business you work in you may well find yourself falling foul of claims of confidentiality, i.e. pillow talk. Even though you spend your night times chatting happily about nothing more innocuous than the price of tea in the supermarket, bosses may well worry that there's business talk going on over the cornflakes, especially if you work for different departments.

And what if your newly found love happens to be a client, or work for a rival company? The complications involved there would be more than obvious and you may find your bosses becoming twitchy in the extreme. The strain of not discussing work may also cause complications in the relationship. One personnel manager was living with a woman from Sales. There had been rumours of redundancies going around the company and the woman's anxiety had reached the point where she was becoming unwell, while all the time her partner knew her job was safe. Should he have told her or not? His behaviour was impeccable and he said nothing, feeling throughout like a complete heel. Did he get any thanks for his virtuous behaviour? No. Furthermore, when the redundancies were announced and his partner's name was not on the list he was accused of favouritism even though the decision had not been his.

You may well then find yourself in a 'no win' situation. Boss/staff affairs are notoriously hard to juggle without accusations of nepotism. Some managers will even err on the side of caution, treating their partner more severely than other staff in an attempt to be scrupulously fair, although I would imagine their home life must be hell for doing so.

Rest assured you will be watched like a hawk by the other staff. The lower-level partner in the relationship will often find their popularity among colleagues sinking to zero because everyone is frightened of behaving naturally or moaning about the boss in their hearing.

Sleeping with the boss is rarely a career-enhancing move in the sleaze-scoured Nineties, where the pressure to be fair is so great that you may find yourself passed over – rather than pushed – for promotion.

Companies used to take a firm line with office romances, either banning them (and marriages) altogether, or letting it be known that they took a very dim view of such carrying on. One major department store, for instance, would insist one partner left the firm when colleagues married. The view used to be that confidentiality was at risk. Nowadays the rules are more relaxed, although some firms still discourage office partnerships and one of the pair may often be surreptitiously relocated or even placed in a different department.

Split-ups

Splitting up can be the most difficult manoeuvre to stage-manage effectively. Not all affairs will end in married bliss and many go painfully down the drain. Splitting up with a partner may be difficult in a social context, but mixing work into the equation can cause nightmare complications.

How often is a split mutual? If a handshake and brief smile of regret has been achieved, then bully for you. I still tend to wonder whether one of the party isn't gritting their teeth just a little too strongly as they smile. And what if the whole thing is acrimonious? Broken hearts don't suit the work culture, and neither does sexual revenge. No matter how brave you try to be it can be almost unbearable to continue seeing the person you loved each and every day once the romance is over.

How will you cope with hearing about, or even working with, their new soulmates? How long before the salt that gets continuously ground into the wound stops stinging? Even if you were the one who called a halt to the relationship it can still be galling to hear your ex whispering sweet nothings down the phone to someone else.

Will you even trust your ex's business loyalty if you were the one who caused the split, leaving them distraught and primed for revenge?

If you are contemplating an office affair then you should always take steps to work out what you will do if it ends. Some people have even quit their jobs because working next to the person who jilted them became unbearable. You may think that would never happen to you, but misery is a powerful emotion, even if you do have a large mortgage to pay.

The One-night Stand

And what about more casual flings? What about the one-night stand? In business the one-night stand just does not exist, if, in fact, it exists at all anywhere. Sex on the hoof just has to be insulting to one or both of the parties. You cannot apply rules to a relationship because relationships are emotion-based. You may know what *you* want but you can never second-guess the other person's feelings. They may agree to a brief fling, but how do you know what they are really hoping for? Even your own emotions may change after sex.

Try as you might, I would challenge anyone not to feel insulted on some level if the lust-bucket of the previous evening doesn't make some move to contact them again the following day. You may not wish to see that person again, but do you really want to feel that you can be dismissed that easily? One-night stands usually leave one party feeling aggrieved, even if you'd need to remove their toenails one at a time to get them to admit it!

Morning Greetings

Seeing that person the next day at work will be difficult. Do you intend to pretend nothing ever happened and resume polite relations? Will you ignore them altogether? Send them flowers with 'Thanks' written on the note? Tell them it was all a dreadful mistake? Agree it was a one-off and shake on the deal? All of this is tacky. Best not to, then.

The Chat-up

Making a pass is a dangerous manoeuvre in the workplace. If your interest is not reciprocated you could be accused of sexual harassment, or – at least – end up looking sad and sleazy once the office gossips have done their worst.

Fancying someone you work with is not a criminal offence and neither is asking them out. It's always wise to keep in mind, though, that in the workplace you should think and plan before you act. Prior to making a play for a colleague work out the following, however hard it is to be coldly rational under the circumstances:

1. Do either of you have any other attachments, i.e. are you or this other person married/living with another? Do either of you have a steady partner? Does that partner work in the same company?
2. What are your positions in the company pecking-order? Are they compatible?
3. Are you in any danger of being accused of favouritism if you start to see each other outside work? Will the charge of confidentiality come up?
4. How highly do you value this person as an employee/colleague/ friend? Will a relationship compromise that situation?
5. What if you see one another and then break up? Will that affect the business relationship?
6. What do you expect the company will think about a romance between the two of you?

Yes, I know you're only going to ask this colleague down the pub, not down the aisle, but it's always best to study every angle of a situation before taking the plunge.

Etiquette

Dating a work colleague requires a good amount of old-fashioned social etiquette, not because it will make you any more attractive but because it will make the whole process a lot more comfortable and a lot less difficult if and when the whole thing ends.

Subtlety is not the wisest ploy. Working with someone means forging an effective relationship. Hinting that you would like to take things further but never being specific can make the relationship uncomfortable, especially if it's a boss/employee situation.

Trying to blur the lines between business and pleasure will appear sleazy. This would entail getting someone to work late at the office and then taking them out for a meal 'because it's too late to go home and cook', or taking them away on a business conference and making sure your rooms are next door to one another. Hedging your bets in this way is mean. Working well with someone means being relaxed with them and that is impossible if you're not sure whether they're trying to seduce you or not.

When someone operates in this manner it is difficult to know when to say 'No, thank you'. If you do tell this colleague you're not interested in them as a partner they may claim – unfairly – that that was never their intention in the first place (ha, ha, ha), craftily extricating themselves from the area of conflict, leaving a sour taste all round.

Being Positive

Surely the best move if you fancy a colleague is to ask them out on a good, old-fashioned date. Let them know it's a social thing too, or they may be unsure whether it's a meeting to discuss business. Be light in tone but clear about your intentions. (No, not all of them, of course.) Allow them to see that you want to put the relationship on a social footing, thereby also allowing them the courtesy of turning you down too.

Plan your next move if they do turn you down. Take 'no' to mean no, and never cajole, push or ask for an explanation. Don't skulk, sulk or become bitter or sarcastic. Plan a semi-jokey line that will immediately alleviate the atmosphere between the two of you and restore normal working relations. You now want me to come up with some appropriate lines for you, don't you?

Simple is best as it avoids too much blush-inducing babble. So how about:

'That's okay. No hard feelings' or
'Wise girl/chap (whatever)' or

'No, you're right. I enjoy working with you, so why complicate things?'

(Put your own tone and inflection onto these. On paper they read a bit like Noel Coward out-takes.)

And at all costs avoid the following:

'That's okay. No hard feelings. As I hope you won't have when I tell you your pay rise has just been cancelled.'

'That's okay, I only asked for a bet.'

'So Quentin in Accounts was right after all, you are/n't lesbian/gay.'

'It's okay, my wife/husband and I have an open marriage.'

Be polite, open, honest and assertive, not furtive. Don't drop hints, or come on too heavy. And never be lewd (good, old-fashioned word) or make a pass. How about:

'Would you like to come out for a meal with me tomorrow night? Purely social, no work to be discussed.'

If you don't like that then write your own script, but make it something along these lines.

Breaking up without Tears

If you find this person is not the man/woman of your dreams it would be cruel to keep things going beyond the first date. Now, remember: all those nasty little tricks people use to ditch someone will be absolutely no use in the workplace. You cannot stand them up or forget to phone. The phrase 'I'll call you' won't apply because you'll see their smiling face next morning in the office. And because of that there must be a rule:

Sex on the first date is OUT!

Think Glenn Close in *Fatal Attraction*, think anything that will scare you enough to persuade you to wait until you are in a serious and stable relationship. This isn't talking killjoy, this is just being practical. Do what you want on the social scene, but in business do not be too eager.

It is difficult jilting anyone you have to work with, but once you have had sex it is a million times tougher and more complicated.

To finish with anyone gracefully you are going to need tact and you are going to need courage. Lying is not a good option, as in: 'I'd love to see you again but I'm afraid I'd end up falling in love with you' or 'My mother has just fallen ill with gout and I will be busy nursing her for the foreseeable future.'

Neither, though, is blatant honesty, as in: 'I thought I fancied you until I saw how you set about that four-course meal' or 'I didn't realise you had absolutely no conversation outside the workings of the fax machine.'

You want me to provide you with some more good lines, don't you? Well, how about 'Thanks for a lovely evening, I only wish we could have done it again some time' and then beat a hasty retreat making it clear that you mean the opposite of what you say. If they insist on pushing you you could productively add: 'Oh, you know my home situation' and if they still ask questions finish with 'I prefer not to talk about it.'

A thank-you note is quite useful as it sounds friendly, formal but final. 'Thank you for a lovely evening. I'll remember it for a long time.'

Or you could be the first one in with 'Thank you for coming to dinner with me last night. I always think it's a good idea to meet work colleagues out of the office now and again, don't you?'

Again, put these ideas into your own words if you don't like the sound of them.

Never ignore the person or lie low for a few days after the date. Never leave them feeling humiliated. They may have told colleagues you were both going out and will not want to lose face in front of the whole office. Which brings me to the next point: be discreet.

Be Discreet

Never welch on a date. Don't tell even your closest workmates what went on. There's no need to keep the whole thing secret but never ever spill the beans about what was said and what was done. Be gallant. Never tell anyone you work with what a disaster/rave it was. Don't discuss details of moles, birthmarks or size of body parts. The excuse you present to your date for not seeing them again should be the same one you give to everyone else.

Word always gets back. Be charming and never inflict unnecessary suffering. If you are asked out by a co-worker and turn them down, keep that quiet too. Don't boast about your pulling power and don't mock the afflicted.

Uncontrollable Passions

There is a strange mental phenomenon that can overpower even the most serious-minded and conscientious employee when they embark on an affair with a colleague, and that is that they suffer a barely controllable urge to get down to having sex at work.

'Why?' you will ask, and the only possible answer is:

It is very naughty.

For grown adults opportunities to be naughty are as rare as hens' teeth. Once your parents become permissive enough to allow you to have sex in their house a whole vista of naughtiness vanishes at one fell swoop. For some folk, the only way to achieve the same furtive, adrenalin-charged experience is either to do it while bungee-jumping or over the office filing cabinet.

For anyone thinking of indulging I will add only five words at this point:

Open-plan offices.

Security cameras.

Need I say more?

If you must indulge, though, here are some of the favourite office spots for consummating that torrid affair:

1. Desktops
   A prime naughty spot on account of the fact that what would normally host hour after hour of sweated slave-labour should also be permitted to induce the odd bout of more fun-filled perspiration. Desktops inspire the ultimate fantasy as business accoutrements are knocked to the floor with one fell swoop of a worsted-clad arm (difficult with all the PC equipment, I know: all those leads and plugs and mouse-mats), buns are unpinned, spectacles torn off, plus all that ice-cold laminated chipboard stretching out beneath you with

just the odd unseen paperclip or stapler to mar the magic of the moment.

2. Stationery cupboards

   Or any cupboards, come to that, and the more cramped the better.

3. Photocopiers

   For all those happy couples wishing to send their friends visual souvenirs of their intimate moments.

4. The roof

   Fire drills *à deux* tend to be popular with the happy couple tripping furtively up the fire escape to the relative privacy of the roof (flat roofs are safer but the more adventurous will swear by the sloping variety). The added advantage of using the roof is that you can get a suntan at the same time.

5. The boss's office

   For members of The Dangerous Sports Club only, unless one of the participants happens to be the boss.

6. The lift

   For speedy practitioners only, unless you enjoy being interrupted by firemen.

7. The car park

   Basement car parks are usually badly lit, which could be an advantage, although stories abound of couples getting stuck ...

CHAPTER 3

Asking for It?

> He didn't look upset when his manager grabbed him at the office party. We all thought he was enjoying it.
>
> She used to flirt like crazy with the guy at the next desk. It was just her way of joking, she was like it with everyone. He was just stupid enough to misread the signals and take it seriously, that's all.
>
> I can honestly say I've never had any trouble with men I work with. I believe you can send out the right and wrong sorts of signals. I look confident and dress smart, so men know I won't be messed around.
>
> *Anonymous*

To stimulate a really raging debate, ask whether a woman in a revealing outfit is 'asking for trouble'.

What – if anything – is provocative behaviour? What happens when dress or body language signals get misinterpreted?

Is a businessman guilty of inappropriate behaviour if he stares at a female colleague's bare midriff? Would I stare at a male colleague's legs if he wore cut-off shorts to work? Everyone has their own answers to questions like these and debating those answers would take for ever. Most theories will begin to look flimsy if pushed to the furthest degree.

Could a man roam the office naked and then tell colleagues off for staring? And yet no behaviour should technically be classified as 'asking for it', apart from doing that very one thing.

Even the 'it' of the catchphrase can have meanings that vary between rape and a stare or comment.

The controversy is not a generational one, either, although different age groups have their own ideas of what is and isn't appropriate business dress or behaviour.

When I interviewed men to elicit tales of female harassment many suggested that female colleagues who strode about the office in revealing outfits were guilty of harassment by default. The men claimed to be aware of the charge of harassment that could be brought if they were caught staring and said inappropriate dress was therefore horribly unfair.

Then there are the less sensitive types.

Take the following situation that was related to me by a City businessman and his wife:

BUSINESSMAN: I had a secretary who used to like to dress in provocative, revealing clothes in the office. She knew I liked that sort of thing and I knew she liked to please me. There was nothing more to it than that.

The other women she worked with found it degrading, though, and came to me to ask her to stop it. I told the secretary I thought she had a fantastic body but that she ought to wear something more appropriate. I didn't want to hurt her feelings.

WIFE: The other girls who worked for him came to me and complained he looked at their boobs when he was talking to them. I told them he can't help it, he does it to everyone, even to me.

So what about these views? Right or Wrong? Discuss!

Was this an innocent and reasonable man falsely accused? Were the women who worked for him a gang of sour-faced prudes or was he a lecherous old oggler?

Business Dress

Workwear in this country is still surprisingly formal for many occupations, but even in traditional companies women have fewer rules about dress than men.

We are in an era of casualisation, but currently the work 'uniform' for most businessmen could be described as navy or grey suit, shirt and tie, flat shoes and socks. The only flesh on display will be the hands, neck and face, apart from the case of the shin-flasher, that is, whose socks part company with the hem of the trouser. Sometimes the arms will be displayed to just above the elbow (big deal) if short-sleeved shirts emerge in summer. Even the business shorts that are offered as an option each summer by many menswear designers become rendered instantly non-seductive by the addition of the usual grey woolly socks on the feet.

Nothing is tight, revealing or unduly suggestive or wanton. Most men will be kitted out in the same manner, whatever their age. Fashion is not a big issue, and neither – apparently – is seduction. Outfits like these could be described as the 'silent' option, because they say very little about the wearer. The only daring business option to date is the bright lycra cycling gear sported by some employees of messenger companies.

Businesswomen have no real 'silent' option. Skirts, trousers, suits, dresses, short, long, on the knee – there's very little that gets the thumbs-down, apart from jeans or leggings. Therefore every garment selected 'speaks' more than those chosen by men.

Fashion variants are more common. Fashion is not understood by everyone. One woman's fashion look is another man's 'She's wearing it to be sexy' look.

Again – as in most things – perceptions will vary. Being revealing is not always an invitation to be groped or stared at. Do builders who sport bum-cleavage do it to turn passers-by on and garner the odd pinch or pat? I suspect not. If a businesswoman accused of staring at a fellow-worker's flies while they spoke claimed he was 'asking for it for wearing a zipper there' would this be valid?

I once ran a training seminar for a group of male scientists who turned up for work in lycra cycling shorts. They claimed their motive was to appear rebelliously non-corporate, rather than to be a turn-on for the women they worked with.

I believe that there are clothes that are inappropriate for businesswear. Too short, too low-cut, too skin-tight, too much underwear showing: I wouldn't describe any of these outfits as 'asking for it' but I would say they were wrong for work.

A balance can be struck by sticking to a dress code that is appropriate for the business you work in. Professional clothes should never send out misleading signals, although some poor, sex-starved individuals will even find a three-piece tweed suit with hand-knitted socks and a thermal vest highly suggestive!

Cultures vary and so do appropriate styles. Little bare flesh is sported in traditional business companies, though in more fashionable media companies it might be the norm for both men and women.

Body Talk

The other non-verbal signals in question come from our body language. What can be rated provocative? Is there such a thing as inappropriate body language? Again, as in business dress, it can all be a matter of culture and perception.

The normal sexual signals – apart from the most blatant, like touching or groping – can all have more than one cause or interpretation, and therefore caution is called for. Body langauge is not a precise science, although some books and articles would have us believe that certain gestures always mean certain things.

You may have read or been told that any or all of the following are a sure sign that someone fancies you:

1. Prolonged eye contact.
2. Smiling.
3. Open gestures.
4. Small grooming movements, like patting or adjusting the hair.
5. Blushing.
6. Holding the head down and looking up with the eyes.
7. Sitting with the legs crossed in your direction.
8. Fingering pens or other equally phallic objects while a man is speaking.
9. Playing with wedding ring.
10. Touching mouth or throat.
11. Both feet pointing straight towards you.
12. Gazing at your mouth while you talk.

However, before you interpret these signals as the green light for passion, perhaps you should consider some possible alternative motives for each action, like:

1. The sender may have undergone sales training, or may simply be keen to impress on you that they are listening.
2. A recommended ploy on customer care courses. Also employed to appear polite.
3. The sender may just be a keen and emphatic talker.
4. Perhaps they just noticed how messy your hair looks, which reminded them about their own. Maybe it was merely windy out.
5. Perhaps your flies are undone.
6. This and the above can both be signs of shyness, rather than lust.
7. There are only two ways to fold the legs. The odds are they'd end up in this position at some stage during the conversation.
8. The listener may be showing boredom, rather than passion.
9. May be caused by ring-rash, which can happen if there is a build-up of soap beneath the metal.
10. May have an itch, or could also be a sign of lying.
11. May just have good posture.
12. You could have spinach between your teeth.

So what, if any, are the subtle signs of attraction? Eye contact is a strong signal, as in 'Their eyes met across a crowded room', although this simple gesture has become devalued, largely through the efforts of customer care courses that insist that the more eye contact you use, the more honest you will look.

And effective eye contact should never be confused with staring, which is a threatening signal, used by many animals to show aggression.

Dilation of the pupils is also supposed to show desire and attraction, and this could be seen as one of the most reliable signals, although heavy drug abuse could have the same effect.

Smiling can't be equated with sexual desire at work because there is an onus upon people to smile more in the workplace. This is called 'masking', employing a facial expression that will look pleasing to the client or colleague in an attempt to impress. This smile should never be confused with the genuine smile of pleasure, which rarely occurs during working hours unless the job is exceptionally stimulating.

At work we tend to succumb to extensive role-play. We are constantly thrown into situations that are alien to us, having to pretend to be someone we aren't or to show feelings that are contrary to our true nature. There is pressure to be nice to difficult colleagues or customers, to fake confidence when we are nervous or unsure, and to react in an appropriately unemotional and professional manner at all times. Therefore no one should fall into the trap of taking business body signals at face value.

Support staff, in particular, may have to act out a role that can be misleading. Bosses expect loyalty, cheerfulness, helpfulness, support, and sometimes will even demand non-business duties, like sewing on buttons, taking clothes to the dry cleaner's, ordering flowers and booking holidays.

The danger arises when this fake role of loyalty and fidelity is mistaken for true affection or intimacy. The boss/worker relationship should never be abused and assumptions should never be made. Devotion to duty is not the same as unadulterated lust or love for the person in charge.

Another reason for thinking twice before making a pass.

CHAPTER 4

Consenting Adults

The modern office is a place where we spend a major
part of our working lives, and we can easily spend more
time with our colleagues than our partners. However, it
can be extremely problematic to have a relationship with
another person at work. It is easy to misinterpret what
colleagues can say and reach the wrong conclusions.
Of course, many happy relationships do start at work,
but it's probably best to look further than the next desk.
Perhaps waiting for the 11.30 Diet Coke break is one
answer?

James Reed, Chief Executive of Reed Personnel Services

Flirting goes on in as well as out of the workplace. An old–fashioned
art that never seems to die out, it can add a little *frisson* of excitement
without the danger of a full-blown affair.

A good flirt gets the balance right without ever overstepping the
mark. An accomplished flirt will keep things at a comfortable level.
Nothing serious is intended but the attraction is implied. Some flirts will
flirt with everyone, whether they find them attractive or not. Flirting
is jokey and safe. If it is practised properly no one should feel threatened
or belittled.

I have encountered business relationships that are built on constant flirtation. In a way it's a kind of mutual flattery. The word *mutual* plays an important role, though. One-sided and constant flirting may look like harassment if it's not wanted or reciprocated.

Flirting is a business technique with a great pedigree. It requires charm and empathy to work. It should never be used as a sexual put-down.

Accomplished flirts will:

● Get people's names right and use them a lot.
● Remember you, even if your original meeting was only fleeting.
● Remember things about you, like the name of your cat or the fact that you don't eat shellfish. (One great flirt of my own acquaintance kept record cards of everyone he met, with these details printed on them. A bit creepy, perhaps, but very effective nevertheless when he recalled someone's star sign three years after the initial conversation.)
● Listen when you speak – immensely flattering.
● Pay subtle, jokey compliments.
● Laugh when you are funny.
● Be happily married or living with a partner (usually).
● Flirt with their husband/wife/partner as well.

The social flirt may also use touch as part of the skill, but the business flirt should not. (See notes on sexual harassment in Chapter 7.)

Where things can go wrong is when the flirting is clumsy or becomes misconstrued for something more serious. It's a finely tuned game that can go pear-shaped if someone forgets the rules. Otherwise it's great. Old can flirt with young and vice versa. Women can flirt and so can men. You don't have to be attractive or powerful to get away with it, it's a game that anyone can join in.

An Open Affair

But what if things are more serious? How do you conduct an office affair with discretion? When, if ever, should you come clean and own up?

The good news is that office affairs, if not exactly encouraged, are no longer considered a hanging offence by many companies, so keeping it hush-hush is not always necessary. The pros and cons of keeping any romance under wraps will still exist, though.

For Being Discreet

● You feel your private life should be just that – private. Blossoming romance is a delicate flower that may wither beneath the scrutiny of the public eye. (Don't worry, that is about as poetic as this book will get.) Or – to put it another way – do you want everyone knowing your business? People will gossip and speculate. You will get asked how things are going on a regular basis. Colleagues will joke about marriage at a stage when you're barely into the first tentative snog. The pressure can kill a relationship stone-dead before it starts.

● Gossip can be harmful. What people don't know they will often make up. This can only apply if they know enough to get them interested.

● You may be accused of nepotism or pillow talk.

● You may both get teased by colleagues.

Against

● Office gossips will probably suss you out anyway. Trying to keep the affair under wraps will only lead them to believe there's something worth gossiping about.

● If the whole thing gets serious you will probably need to confess your love at some time. Colleagues may feel peeved that you could keep the whole thing to yourself for so long. Didn't you trust them to be discreet? The answer is probably 'no', but tact will be needed. They may think you have other things you are keeping from them. They may start to look at you from out of the corners of their eyes in future.

● People love a good drama. If you keep your affair under wraps you will deny your poor bored colleagues a good source of daily entertainment.

Wedding Bells

Office marriages can be the stuff of dreams or nightmares. Collections will be made and the entire office will expect to be invited to the big day itself. Imagine the horror of looking back down the pews and seeing the entire population of your open-plan office togged out in ill-fitting suits. Do you want a life outside business? Then marry a folk singer or astronaut instead.

Then there is the question of the shared surname. Does the woman comply with convention and take her husband's name? Will two people with the same name cause identification problems in the office? What about the amount of effort caused by changing names on the paperwork and telephone listings? Better to keep single names, then. But then you have the problem of The Client/Colleague Who Doesn't Know, and who bitches about your spouse in your waiting ear. At what point do you tell them that it is your dearest heart they are slagging off? Or do you avoid a confession and let them find out from a colleague later?

And what sort of body language do newly-marrieds indulge in at work? This will need choreography. Either the sexual signals are going to be there for all to see, in which case colleagues will have fun spotting the moment when the passion dies down a bit, or it will be business as usual and you give your partner barely a passing glance as your paths cross in the corridor.

If you want to know how to get the balance right you could do no worse than watch morning TV, which seems to have an endless supply of marrieds or non-marrieds sitting together on settees and simulating married couple chemistry. The role models are there in abundance as a guideline to current etiquette.

For those unable to tune in at that hour, I can only pass on from the fleeting moments I have caught myself that the tip seems to be to not sit too close, to bicker now and again in a light-hearted way, to exchange glances occasionally and to smack one another sharply across the knee in a playful fashion when the banter gets a bit too ripe.

CHAPTER 5

Rules of Engagement

You never know how to treat women in business these days. Some like to have doors opened for them, while others will bite your head off and accuse you of being sexist. All I am is old-fashioned and think a lady should be treated with respect.

Some guy I worked for insisted on carrying all my bags and books for me and hopping around trying to get the door. We used to bump into each other all the time. I told him there was no need. One day he let me open a door for him and I felt I'd really achieved something.

Anonymous

What about the great unmarrieds of office life, though? If behaviour between couples can be difficult at work, how about the new etiquette rules for colleagues of the opposite sex?

Most business etiquette has been founded on the same rules as old social etiquette, the premise being that women are creatures from another planet who are both physically and mentally weaker than their male counterparts. Women don't swear or talk about football or sex. They have no bones in their arms and are therefore incapable of opening doors without male assistance. Their main role at work is a decorative one and their choice of dress should reflect that.

This is, of course, bunkum. Women swear and they talk dirty. Not all women, but then neither do all men. The best way to treat men and women in business is as equals.

Avoid making assumptions. A woman is as likely to object to swearing as a man. A woman may be weaker than some men but she may also be stronger than others. Women should not be treated as a special case and they shouldn't expect to be, either. Each person in business should be judged on individual merits and weaknesses, regardless of sex.

Equals

This unbiased perception would be easier if the workplace was historically even-handed, but unfortunately it isn't. In many professions, men got there first. Women arrived rather late on the business scene and by then a lot of damage had already been done. Despite many notable exceptions, industry still tends to be run by men.

So stop the soppy, outdated business etiquette and bring on some new guidelines. I would like to see:

- Women referred to as women, rather than 'ladies', 'girls', 'girlies', etc.
- The term 'Ms' used on a widespread basis. Why should women have to inform all and sundry in business about their marital status? A female form of 'Mr' is the logical conclusion and 'Ms' is the front-runner at the moment (in fact, it's about the only one in the field). If you don't like it, tough. It's only a tiny, two-letter word and so there is no need to cause such a fuss. It's not hard to say after a bit of practice and it will put an end to all those embarrassed and gloriously unnecessary enquiries about whether a businesswoman has been escorted down the aisle or not.

  If women insist on using the Mrs/Miss form of address then we should act equally by referring to businessmen as 'Master' until they've done the nuptial bit.
- No one expecting a female colleague to pour the coffee at a business meeting. And yet I see women gleefully throwing themselves on the pot, yelling 'I'll be mother.' This is called colluding in a negative stereotype.
- No one assuming that the woman on the other end of the phone is someone's secretary.

- Women employing the handshake on a regular basis when meeting and greeting.
- Neither men nor women making sexist remarks.
- Businesswomen who travel feeling comfortable about going down to the hotel restaurant for a meal by themselves in the evening and eating without reading a book at the same time.

Curses

Swearing at work is a very tricky subject. Like sex, you know you shouldn't do it, but then a lot of people do. When you swear in front of other people you are either showing a disregard of their feelings or you are making assumptions about what they will find acceptable.

Everyone has their own idea of what words are or aren't acceptable and – let's face it – there are always some people who will find *all* bad language, even the mildest stuff, totally offensive. So should all these po-faced colleagues take themselves off to a monastery or nunnery, leaving the office air to turn blue with unfettered abandon or should all swearing be banned instead?

Again, the whole issue hinges on perception, culture and upbringing. And never assuming that other people don't mind bad language just because they don't react when you use it. Not everyone winces visibly when they're offended and not everyone is assertive enough to voice a complaint out loud, either. Silence should never be seen as a green light to continue or get worse.

A few suggested guidelines, then:

1. Never swear in front of a client
   Just don't. Not even if they do. And definitely don't if they don't. And I'm not just talking about the hard-core stuff here, either. You won't know their religious predilections and even the use of words like 'God!' or 'Christ almighty!' may cause deep offence. It won't hurt too much to keep your language clean when you're dealing with customers or clients. Just be professional.
2. Don't 'catch' swearing
   If you work in one of those business cultures where swearing is considered the norm there is no need for you to feel pressured to join in, unless you want to.

3. Swearing by degrees
   Swearing at work will come under different categories:
   a) Kids' stuff
      Naughty little words or phrases like 'naffed off', 'blinking awful'
      or 'bloody great' shouldn't really cause an attack of the vapours
      in anyone old enough to vote. If you happen to notice that one
      of your colleagues hand-crochets bedjackets as a hobby, though,
      you could be wise to use your discretion in future!
   b) Strong-ish but seemingly unavoidable
      You know the sort of thing. You drop that heavy file on your toe or
      get an engaged tone on the phone for the fortieth time of ringing.
      Would anyone expect you to cry out 'Oh dearie, dearie me!'? Prob-
      ably not. There are times when only a good, air-renting curse will do.
         However, you should still proceed with caution. Apologise
      afterwards. When in doubt stuff your fist into your mouth and
      take yourself off to the loo before letting rip. It's not nice and
      it's not clever, however unavoidable it may seem.
   c) Casual and frequent
      This is the sort of ripe stuff that gets ingrained into the culture
      of a workplace to the point where it becomes the norm. Or it
      may just be you who is a frequent user, 'f—ing' your way about
      the office in true blue liberated fashion.
         Use caution. People may forgive the odd swear word used
      under duress but the casually employed stuff is always more
      offensive. Just because the words are the norm in your own
      vocabulary you should never consider them generally inoffensive.
      Frequency doesn't dull the blow. Apologising after each salvo will
      be tedious and repetitious.
   d) Personal attack
      Swearing at a colleague is unacceptable. This is a major act of
      aggression and can never be considered professional behaviour.
      Worst of the lot is the boss who swears at their staff. Managers who
      manage their staff well will never have any need to swear at them.
      Any constructive criticism will be lost in the wake of the insult.
      Being sworn at hurts. Don't even think about it.
   e) The 'Not when there's ladies present' variety
      This is horribly patronising. A man either swears or goes to swear

at work and then checks himself out loud by claiming 'There are ladies present'. If he had an atom of good manners he would never have sworn in the first place. This behaviour also suggests that all men are foul-mouthed brutes who are only barely able to contain their animalistic urges because members of the fairer sex are present. It also implies that women never swear, which is f—ing ridiculous.

f) The joke swear

For some reason people who would never use bad language at work seem to feel it's okay when they're telling a joke to colleagues. Humour does diffuse a lot of otherwise offensive language, but coyly starting the joke by apologising for your language in advance doesn't really make it okay.

CHAPTER 6

Body Contact

> **He acted as though we were big pals together and said I was silly if I thought he had an ulterior motive. He said I'd got it all wrong.**
>
> *25-year-old woman who was awarded £12,900 compensation for constructive dismissal*

With non-verbal communications forming about 55 per cent of the perceived message when we deal with an individual face-to-face, body language signals can range from the appropriate to the downright intimidating.

Remember that your gestures, facial expressions, touch and use of personal space will all create high-impact, silent indications that will affect those around you on both conscious and subconscious levels.

Eye Level

The eyes are powerful communicators. Staring, as we all know, is usually classed as insulting. Staring starts fights in pubs: 'Are you looking at me?' 'Were you staring at my bird?' 'Wot's your trouble, pal?' etc.

Staring in crowded public places, like tube trains or lifts, is out. Even a brief meeting of eyes can be embarrassing under these circumstances.

The British are particularly wary of eye contact and will often fail to use it when greeting, shaking hands or exchanging business cards. A long stare is considered threatening. Staring at parts of the body could obviously be classed as sexual harassment, but then so can staring at the face or into the eyes, if it makes the victim feel uncomfortable. It isn't natural, under the law of animal behaviour. Some people claim they can't help staring or other inappropriate behaviour. 'I'm not even aware I'm doing it' etc. Well, pull the other one, matey.

The easiest way to judge whether inappropriate behaviour is avoidable or not is to see whether the culprit does it to:

a) The boss.
b) Clients.
c) Members of their own sex, especially large, potentially aggressive-looking members of their own sex.

Would he gaze at the managing director's chest as she strolled through the office?

Would she touch a male colleague's thigh when she was in a business meeting?

Would he scratch himself like that in front of a client?

Behaviour can always be modified, and staring is no exception. If it makes your colleagues feel uncomfortable – as it no doubt will if it is inappropriate – then cut it out.

Space Wars

We all have our own 'comfort zone', which is the space around our bodies that is a no-go area to all but our nearest and dearest. It is the 'touching distance', that inner circle of territory that is so slender that anyone entering it will be almost certain to touch us.

In the UK this 'intimate zone' extends about eighteen inches from the body. Some other cultures are happily tactile but we are not. Anyone entering this zone uninvited will therefore be seen as a threat.

If you live in a city the odds are your intimate zone is breached on a daily basis as you commute to work. On trains and buses we are forced into a crush that leads to touch and closeness with people we have never met, let alone been introduced to. This is where the 'emergency procedure' comes into play. Because your spatial behaviour is forced to become inappropriate you signal your own lack of threat or aggression in three ways:

1. Lack of eye contact.
2. Lack of body signals.
3. Lack of facial expression.

In a way, you try to cease to exist. If you sat in the same way in your office your colleagues would be extremely disturbed by your behaviour.

Spatial zones are easily breached in business but the result will often be discomfort for one of the parties. The zones are closely linked with ownership of territory. Sitting on the edge of someone's desk, for example, could cause distress because not only are you invading their territory, in a way you're claiming it for yourself too. Leaning over someone's shoulder while they're working is another way to cause discomfort, as is sitting too close while you are talking, even during a meeting.

Many managers have pondered long and hard over the appropriate form of seating during a meeting or interview. Sitting on both sides of a desk is seen as challenging, or creating a barrier, and in many ways this is true.

But at the same time the desk forms a comfort zone that can lead to unease when it is missing. Is it more difficult to be interviewed with a desk between you and your interviewer, or with no 'safety barrier' at all? Sometimes interviewers go too far in their attempt to make the interviewee feel at ease, ending up creating the opposite effect.

Chatting to someone while sitting in low-slung settees and nearly within touching distance can be extremely distressing. This is really 'social sitting' and may not work in business. Delegates on a training course will often admit to feeling 'comfortable' sitting behind desks but 'exposed' or slightly 'threatened' if the desks are removed so that no barriers exist between them and the lecturer.

A speaker on stage would do well to step away from a lectern or table to create unrestricted communication with the audience, but that same lack of restriction can make one-to-one communications difficult, which is why a low table, such as a coffee table, will often be introduced. This subtle barrier means movement is possible without risk of touch, and places both individuals back inside their own 'comfort zone'.

'Lurking' is unattractive business behaviour, and so is 'looming', which can be threatening. Lurkers often operate out of the best of intentions, politely side-lining themselves until the person whose attention they require is free, but causing consternation in the process. There is a rule of business behaviour that the more you try to render yourself invisible the more obviously noticeable you become, as in the 'creeping into a busy meeting with the tray of tea' or the 'arriving late but tiptoeing to my desk' syndromes.

Lurkers are unavoidably, spectacularly conspicuous and become even more annoying when you are forced to cease work to ask what they want, only to be told that they will 'wait until you're finished'.

Loomers form less of an annoyance and more of a threat. They stand too close for comfort. This may be a power gesture, a sexual technique or even a sign of cultural diversity but – whatever the reason – it can cause discomfort to the recipient. Always keep a respectful distance when you speak to colleagues. Don't invade their space, even if you're just trying to be friendly.

Keeping in Touch

There is only one safe and appropriate way to touch in business: the handshake, although some people can even inject a little *frisson* of lust into that most polite of gestures with a variety of little extra-curricula touches like wiggling fingers or the surreptitious squeeze.

Sad cases apart, remember:

1. All touch sends out powerful signals, and
2. The UK is a seriously non-tactile country.

We can just about cope with the handshake. Anything more intimate in business may require the services of victim counselling. Even the non-sexual two-handed clasp makes us queasy, so do not at any stage contemplate going European with the De Gaulle air-kiss or the Helmut Kohl hug. In the UK you would have to be engaged to someone before such intimate manoeuvres would even be contemplated.

'But I'm a tactile person!' is the cry of the man/woman who makes their colleagues nervy. Perhaps you came from a huggy, kissy family. Maybe your upbringing *was* healthily tactile. Hugging and squeezing colleagues at work is not on, though. And don't try to tell me you can't help it, it's just the kind of guy/girl you are. Do you do it on tube trains or buses too? If not, you obviously have full control over your body movement. If you do, however, you are probably reading this in prison!

Hugging is only comfortable when we trust the person hugging us, which is why it is usually confined to friends and family or thespian-based professions. Hugging at work is a whole different ball game. How can you tell if the hugged colleague minds or not? Hugging and touching are a severe breach of space, territory and business etiquette, and yet people rarely have the courage to voice their discomfort.

Unwanted touch often evokes embarrassment in the huggee. This could well lead to a facial contortion known as 'the flustered smile', which should never be confused with collusion or encouragement. Just because no one complains, you should never consider this appropriate behaviour.

In British etiquette the following touching may be employed in extreme circumstances in business:

1. The Air-kiss
   (Mainly woman-to-woman in client relationships where social disclosures have been exchanged.)
2. The Manly Hug
   (Ditto for men, but accompanied by much heavy-duty back-punching to show lack of ulterior motive.)
3. The Brief Forearm Touch
   (For use on colleague suffering personal problems.)
4. The Back-pat
   (Brief but friendly form of congratulation.)
5. The High-five Hit
   (Ditto.)
6. The Swift Arm-punch
   (Ditto.)

For Certain Professions Only:

1. Profuse Huggy Greetings
   (Media- or actor-based professions only.)
2. Cupped Hand to Other's Face
   (Medical-based caring professions only.)

3. The Two-handed Shake
   (Doorstepping politicians, although still not recommended as appropriate.)
4. Arm-holding Handshakes
   (Heavy-duty salesmen, although, again, not to be recommended.)
5. Foot-touching
   (Chiropody only.)

Strictly Out of Bounds and Yet Still Regularly Documented:

1. Shoulder-hugging
   (Possibly matey but potenially dodgy.)
2. Total-torso Body Squeezing
   (Creating a small gap in doorways or past filing cabinets by blocking with own body and forcing victim to squeeze through.)
3. Bottom-patting
   (Forget it – under *no* circumstances.)
4. Thigh-patting
   (Ditto.)
5. Hand-holding
   (There are many other ways of getting someone's attention.)
6. Bosom-brushing
   (Did you really think anyone would believe it was accidental?)
7. Leg-brushing
   (Ditto.)

CHAPTER 7

On the Make

I worked for the same company for two years and my career was going well. Then I fell in love with Brian, my boss. I was unattached and he was separated from his wife. He fell for me too, so I thought there would be no harm in starting an affair. We were discreet but some people in the office started to guess something was going on. I had no idea how much trouble could be caused. I worked hard and gained a well-earned promotion that had nothing at all to do with Brian. Unfortunately not everyone seemed to realise that. Word got around that I was only promoted because of the affair. It was probably jealousy but it hurt all the same. Everyone knew how much studying I had put in but they all seemed to prefer to believe I didn't deserve it. In the end I couldn't stand it and I had to leave before my career was destroyed.

Anonymous

In 1993 The Industrial Society carried out a survey which indicated that 54 per cent of working women and 15 per cent of working men had experienced some form of sexual harassment in the workplace.

There is legal protection for victims. Sexual harassment is unlawful under the terms of The Sex Discrimination Act 1975. The EU have also issued a code on measures to combat sexual harassment and this is taken into account by tribunals.

Sexual harassment has become the business bogeyman/woman for many working cultures. The sensitive are terrified of making one inadvertent false move. The guilty cite cases of overblown political correctness to prove matters have been taken too far and claim a little healthy groping here and there would keep us all out of the madhouse.

Anyone can be a victim of sexual harassment. Men as well as women fall foul of inappropriate behaviour and men and women can both be considered victims if they happen to be unfairly accused.

In the bid to blame the guilty the innocent may also suffer. Lurid tales hit the headlines and suddenly every man is seen as potentially predatory, while all women are victims.

Striking a balance is difficult. Again, perception comes into the equation. Cases that are brought to law will always arouse controversy. Behaviour might be wrong but the punishment may be seen to be out of proportion. But who is to decide how severe the crime is? What sends one person reaching for the smelling salts may drive another to loud guffaws of derisive laughter. Many women are quite capable of taking care of themselves in a majority of situations, and some feel threatened by the fact that the courts become involved in relatively minor transgressions, as this could imply women are still very much the weaker sex.

And what about men who are sexually harassed? Does it have to be 'all in a day's work' just because it is discussed less commonly? Would a man who has had his bottom felt by his boss expect sympathy from his colleagues or friends? Perhaps men have been putting up and shutting up for years because they have been taught to use a different perception. Perhaps they're at a point that women reached before the days of Women's Lib, when it was almost considered flattering to be groped or propositioned at work.

Defining the Rules

So what constitutes sexual harassment at work? In their Harassment Policy document, Railtrack define harassment as 'any unwanted conduct affecting the dignity of women and men at work. It includes unwelcome physical, verbal or non-verbal conduct and can amount to unlawful discrimination. It can involve a single incident or may be persistent and may be directed towards one or more individuals.

Unacceptable behaviour includes:

● Unwanted physical conduct such as unnecessary touching, patting, pinching, brushing against another person's body, insulting or abusive behaviour or gestures, physical threats, assault, coerced sexual intercourse or rape.

● Unwanted verbal conduct such as unwelcome advances, patronising titles or nicknames, propositions or remarks, innuendoes, lewd comments, jokes, banter or abusive language which refers to a person's or a group's gender, colour, race, nationality, ethnic or national origins, disability, sexual preference etc., repeated suggestions for unwanted social activities inside or outside the workplace.

● Unwanted non-verbal conduct such as racially or sexually based graffiti or graffiti referring to an individual's characteristics or private life, abusive or offensive gestures, leering, whistling, display of pornographic or suggestive literature, pictures or films/videos or inappropriate use of visual display units or network systems for this purpose.'

In their *Guidance Notes for Managers*, Railtrack also note:

'Harassment is a health and safety issue. It is difficult for anyone who feels under pressure from such treatment to function effectively at work or at home. Under stress and preoccupied by problems, it is all too easy to lose concentration and make mistakes, possibly causing accidents and injuries.'

Male Bonding

When researching this book I asked many working men whether they had ever been harassed in the workplace and the stock response was something along the lines of 'I wish!', or a lot of mocking laughter. Not one man volunteered the fact that he had, and most denials were emphatic and instant. Yet when quizzed a little further it seemed many

of them had been harassed within the strictest definition of the term.
It was just that they didn't *view* the behaviour as harassment. To most
of them it was just a bit of a laugh. The worst emotion was the
embarrassment induced by the telling of the tale. Very few of them felt
threatened by the behaviour. Yet if they had been women describing the
treatment they'd received the harassment would have been obvious.

It is a myth, though, that only men make sexual harassers. Women
can be just as feral, and may get away with more because the victims
may expect less sympathy. Some women even feel the harassment is
justified, under the premise of 'setting the record straight'. One guy I
interviewed had his shirt torn off by female co-workers at a Christmas
party. He said he didn't want this to happen but felt pressured to see
the incident as a bit of a laugh.

Sean, a City PR who is now in his thirties, worked for a woman
boss while in his twenties.

'She owned the company and employed nearly all women. I was one
of only two men in a staff of twenty-four. She would often make
jokey references to having sex with me but I didn't take it seriously.
Then she got drunk at the Christmas party and I was forced to hide
while she went around scouring the place for me'.

A couple of weeks later she came back drunk from a business
lunch and called me into her office. She started telling me how good
she was in bed, and saying every man should try sex with an older
woman at least once in his life.

It was her secretary who rescued me. She was a mature woman
and very sensible. She knew what was going on and came in to say
I had an urgent phone call. I owe her one. The situation was getting
very difficult. The woman was my boss, after all.'

What is Sexual Harassment?

Sexual harassment is bullying of the worst kind and most companies are
at great pains to stamp it out.

The Industrial Society define sexual harassment as '... offensive and
humiliating behaviour of a sexual nature which is uninvited and
unwelcomed by the person at whom it is directed.

It may be expressed:

- Physically.
- Verbally.
- Through body language.
- On paper or screen, either through letters or through the display of sexually suggestive or explicit material.

Sexual harassment has nothing to do with reciprocal romantic or flirtatious relationships between two people.'

The Institute of Personnel and Development describe harassment as:

'Unwanted behaviour which a person finds intimidating, upsetting, embarrassing, humiliating or offensive. It is essential to remember that it is not the intention of the perpetrator that is key in deciding whether harassment has occurred but whether the behaviour is unacceptable by normal standards and disadvantageous. It is also important to distinguish harassment from sexual relationships freely entered into and acceptable to those involved.'

Describing harassment generally in business, they cite forms of it as including:

- Physical conduct.
- Jokes, offensive language, gossip, slander, sectarian songs and letters.
- Posters, graffiti, obscene gestures, flags, bunting and emblems.
- Isolation or non-cooperation and exclusion from social activities.
- Coercion for sexual favours and pressure to participate in political/ religious groups.
- Intrusion by pestering, spying and stalking.

Defining sexual harassment in more personal terms is tricky because it is obviously subjective. Many large companies use the phrase 'would be regarded by any *reasonable* person' – or words to that effect – when describing the parameters of acceptable behaviour. But any swift head-count of 'normal' people will reveal a wide margin of tolerance levels.

Opinions of acceptability vary so much that it is obviously natural to err on the side of caution. We can't read other people's minds. We often don't even know what's going on in our *own* minds. Our perceptions can fluctuate wildly as there is no precise standard of human behaviour.

Do we need to be educated, then, in how to recognise sexual harassment? Should opinions be standard or is flexibility vital? Extremes of inappropriate behaviour are relatively easy to gauge. Most people know when they've been groped or compromised. But what about the more marginal crimes?

Would you consider you had been sexually harassed if a member of the opposite sex winked at you? Your reply to this question will vary depending on your age, gender, culture, and even area of upbringing. Where I was born and brought up (South London) winking was a normal gesture of matiness or friendship, not a predatory sexual innuendo. Wolf-whistles used to make us laugh. I didn't feel victimised by them.

But I also understand that that is only *my* upbringing and *my* opinion. I would hope I could respect the opinion of anyone who felt otherwise. Especially if they worked for me.

A Manager's Role

Being a manager does not give you instant *droit de seigneur* around the office. And yet many bosses seem to feel that the odd titillation is part of the perks. Being a manager makes appropriate behaviour even more crucial because as a manager you have the opportunity to abuse your own power. Staff are unable to respond in a normal way to their manager because the manager may well hold their future livelihood in their hands. Because people are forced to be polite to you, as a manager, there is no reason to assume they lust after, or even *like,* you.

Managers must be above reproach in their behaviour, and they should also ensure that there is no sexual bullying going on further down the line either.

There's nothing difficult about this. You don't *need* to live in mortal fear of saying or doing something untoward. Just keep that rampant sex-god side of your nature in check until you get home, that's all. Was it ever in the job description in the first place? I thought not.

Staff are nice to managers because they want to keep their jobs, and because they want to please. This is the power you have. And yes, your staff may well appear to be far nicer and far more understanding than your spouse at home. But your husband or wife doesn't live in fear of being made redundant by you. In marriage it's called by another name – divorce – and whereas in business you are left without a wage, in marriage divorce means that you may walk out with up to half of your money, rather than empty-handed. The same fear factor isn't there. Partners are only nice to you because they like you. Staff have to be nice to you whether they like you or not.

So – don't take advantage of the situation. You may know you're a nice man/woman with honourable intentions but it's horribly easy for signals to be misinterpreted. For every man or woman who says their boss compromised them there's probably a manager claiming they thought they got the come-on. Niceness and flattery get confused for the real thing.

Masking

At work we wear all sorts of masks, hiding real emotions in a bid to appear professional. The signals are not the same as they are in the social situation. Assertiveness courses are a regular part of modern business life, with delegates desperate to learn how to say 'no' to their customers or their bosses. Keep this in mind and make sure you don't use passivity to your advantage.

Unless you are absolutely sure your feelings are reciprocated, exercise caution. 'Careless talk costs lives' and constant hints and innuendoes will be stressful at the very least. Outright passes cause problems involving your career as well as theirs.

If in doubt, ask the individual out on a straight-forward, honest-to-goodness date, and if they say 'no', go out of your way to show that the refusal will not affect your working relationship. No member of staff should ever feel that by turning your request down they will in any way be compromising their career. (Or enhancing it by saying 'yes', come to that.)

Predatory Behaviour

Even the mildest behaviour can become predatory if displayed too often or in a certain manner. For instance, there is a subtle visual difference between a smile and a leer, and yet the messages sent and received from each will vary tremendously. Staring can be threatening if it is too intense and yet there's nothing wrong with using emphasised eye contact to show you are listening to someone.

The odd innuendo can be funny but a constant barrage is often tiresome and/or inappropriate. A touch on the arm may appear relatively inoffensive when others are around but may become much more worrying if you're working late alone together in a deserted office.

Again, all things are relative. I have seen colleagues laughing at a bad-taste joke using ripe language yet complaining about a much milder one which wasn't as funny.

How to Cope

So what if you feel you are a victim of sexual harassment? There are a variety of options available but it is up to you to choose which is appropriate. I mentioned that some people will feel they need educating as to what is and what isn't sexual harassment.

It's easy to advise that 'it is only harassment if you feel it to be so'. Yet when *I* started work there were all sorts of behaviours that I considered 'normal', including being groped by the boss. It was just something he did. We all laughed about it when his back was turned. The groping included sliding hands inside clothes, and yet all we did was laugh.

Draw your own conclusions from this. All I can say is that we were young and inexperienced and felt our response was sophisticated because we laughed, rather than overreacting hysterically or fearfully. We would have considered any other response to be uncool and unworldly. We felt strangely in control of the situation. This was before Women's Lib kicked in properly: our liberation came because we did not go off screaming and swooning like Victorian ladies, but instead took it all in our stride.

Did we need educating to realise that this groping was gruesome and inappropriate behaviour? I imagine we did, because I look back on it now with a mixture of horror and amusement. And there is no doubt some behaviour that I expect some people would think I need 'educating out of'!

I still take a relatively relaxed view of conduct that others might find intolerable, because this is my current perspective. Whereas my old view was tinged by inexperience, my current opinions rely a lot on acquired knowledge and the fact that I am very much in control of my own career.

Yet I wonder if it feels very much different for young people in their first job today. I would like to believe that they would be less likely to tolerate behaviour similar to that I encountered, yet bullying is on the increase (or at least reported cases are) and most sexual harassment is a form of bullying. So, some guidelines:

- If you *feel* a behaviour is wrong and you have asked for it to stop then it *is* wrong if it continues.
- If you're not sure whether the behaviour in question should bother you or not, ask the advice of a mature-minded friend.
- If you're unhappy about the behaviour you have the right to ask for it to stop, even if you're not sure whether it is 'normal' or not.
- Don't be fobbed off with the lines: 'I didn't mean it like that' or 'I was only joking' or 'You're reading more into it than you should, I was only being friendly'. These stock phrases are as old as mankind. They only work if they come with a sincere apology attached and the behaviour is never repeated.
- Men are allowed to feel uncomfortable or humiliated by sexual harassment. Just because your mates find it funny doesn't mean that you have to tolerate it. It is a form of bullying, whatever the sex of the person doing it. Don't think that because you feel humiliated or embarrassed the only way to cope without losing face is to collude. You have as much right as any woman to say 'no' if you want to.
- Sexual harassment doesn't just mean touching. It can also mean words or looks.
- The sooner you deal with it the better. Dealing with behaviour that has become the norm is more difficult than dealing with it the minute it breaks out. It often means your response can be less severe too.

Potential Responses

Potential responses fall roughly into two categories: The Knee-jerk Emotive Reaction or The Planned and Objective-led Response. Because there is a lot at stake on both sides the planned, measured response is to be recommended.

Here are a few of the pros and cons:

The Knee-jerk Reaction

Instant Retaliation

Of the 'He/she did it to me so I just did it back to them' school of thought.

Rewarding though this response may seem it should never really be seen as an option. Tit for tat generally leads to open warfare and, although no one likes to be seen as a wimp, there are more measured and intelligent strategies to be considered first. Yet this is the one I hear most commonly recommended from one colleague to another, as in: 'If he stares at your boobs you just stare back at the flies of his trousers. See how he likes it.' There is a whole heap of kudos attached to this response because the retaliation is instant and fair; because you gave no more than you got.

This scheme, however, comes under the 'most bullies are cowards' heading, which is dangerously flawed.

It is a myth that, if cornered, all bullies break down and cry for their mothers. Retaliation could be seen as collusion and you may be playing a dangerous game. Perhaps the individual concerned likes having their bum felt by return post. If you brazen it out you could get in deeper than you wanted. The perpetrator may not back down at all. Did you think of a next move if they don't? And if you *do* have to take your complaint to a higher authority, how will it sound if you matched leer for leer and grope for grope?

Planned Retaliation

You decide to exact your revenge in more subtle ways, then, ruining the perpetrator's work, or passing gossip about them around the office. This is, again, rewarding in the short term, but the consequences could be disastrous. If your plot is uncovered you'll need to prove why you were doing it and this could be extremely difficult. And why become a snarling, manipulative person just because this other sleaze decided to go for the grope? The offending behaviour was bad but emulating it will only make your victimisation worse.

Passivity

You can, of course, do nothing at all. This is your decision and it has to be an option. Just realise that bad behaviour that isn't stopped rarely stops by itself.

Third-party Retaliation

As in phoning their husband/wife to inform them just what a sleazebag they are married to. This is not to be recommended, for obvious reasons, because you will be doing the most harm to an innocent party, i.e. the husband or wife, let alone your own career.

Instant Anger

Turning around and yelling or screaming in front of others may mean you end up with more people feeling sympathy for the perpetrator than they do for you, the victim. Also, you will run the risk of being thought hysterical in the workplace.

Tears

Try not to have a sob, as this implies weakness and negates all attempts at a more assertive response, on account of a red, blotchy face, quivering-jelly chin, warbling voice, etc.

A Family Act

Business-based problems are best dealt with by either yourself or a higher authority at work. Getting friends and family to sort it out for you is not a viable option.

The Planned Response

Plain Speaking

You have rights. When the behaviour is unacceptable there is nothing wrong with telling the perpetrator. Plan ahead, though. Nip the problem in the bud by making your feelings known as soon as possible, but – if you have time to plan – sort out when, how and why first. What do you want to gain from your actions? Do you want an apology? The behaviour stopped? Ritual public humiliation of the perpetrator? Rivers of blood? The sack for the perpetrator? Has this behaviour led to *your* job being terminated or the offer of a job held in check? Do you want financial recompense?

Know what you consider to be fair under the circumstances. You may have other objectives, too. Perhaps you still want to be friends with this person. Maybe you want to continue a good working relationship. All these things should be taken into consideration.

As a first step it might be wise to make your feelings felt when you are alone, rather than in front of other colleagues. A lot will depend on the severity of the offence. Taking a determined groper to one side so you can be alone with them may be what is known technically as 'a very bad move'. Less blatant behaviour, though, where you don't feel under physical threat, might be better brought up in private.

Ask to speak to this person at a mutually convenient time and be firm as you do so. Tell them that you find this behaviour inappropriate. Feel free to tell them how upset/angry it makes you too, but try to do it without a big accompanying portion of visible emotion.

Use assertive gestures and eye contact to show your 'no' is non-negotiable. If they try the old soldier routine and start harping on about 'Can't you take a joke?' you could say that of course you can, but show by your expression that you didn't find this funny. Avoid the use of threats at this stage.

Making a Joke

Laughter is a great way to diffuse a situation and put-downs will often sound better if they are funny. I like the humour option, although there are obviously times when it would not be appropriate, e.g. in the case of outright rape or otherwise threatening behaviour.

If you have the gift of the good line you have a built-in protector. Humour is largely non-confrontational and many kids use it in school to help avoid being picked on by a bully. To pull it off, though, you do need a quick wit and a skill for the one-liner. Trying to be funny when you don't have the talent can be dangerous as the words may sound more offensive when unaccompanied by laughter.

Humour is a first-line defence policy. You can't keep cracking jokes if the behaviour you want stopped is incessant. Also the joke shouldn't be too insulting, or the behaviour may become even more vicious.

Dropping Hints

Why drop hints? If you have to say 'no' it is better to be direct. Anyone insensitive enough to harass sexually will probably be completely immune to hints, anyway.

Keeping Clear

If you feel in any physical danger keep clear of the person offending. Try to make sure you are accompanied whenever you are with them and start keeping a log of any bad behaviour. Get witnesses if possible.

Confrontation is not to be recommended in these circumstances. You will have to go to a higher authority, and as quickly as possible. Even so, make sure you are clear with your case before reporting the harasser. Be assertive when you supply details, as threatening behaviour can often sound trivial when it is described out loud.

When you report this behaviour to a superior keep a copy of anything put in writing and log the time and nature of your complaint. If nothing is done keep pushing.

The Layered Response

Unfortunately you may find yourself having to work your way through all the above responses if at first you don't succeed. I think it is generally better to start with humour and work your way to a higher authority, rather than going straight to the boss at the first sign of trouble. Unless the harassment is severe, that is. If it is very severe you may even need to go straight to the police.

Always remember that there is no need for you to tolerate harassment just because other colleagues do. It may be *their* decision to put up and shut up, or even to laugh about the situation, but this doesn't mean that that has to be your choice of action as well.

You may even be told that this person is 'very nice really', or that 'he or she doesn't mean it'. Nice people use nice behaviour; that's how we know that they're nice. Unpleasant behaviour comes from unpleasant people and if you're not happy with it you have every right to complain.

Suffering in Silence

Reasons people are reluctant to complain about harassment include:

● Reluctance to draw attention to the situation.
● Embarrassment.
● Worry about being seen as a victim.
● Doubts that any action will be taken.

- Worry that word will get straight back to the harasser, who may then become worse.
- Worry that others at work will turn against them.
- Concern that they are overreacting.
- The harasser is the boss and their job may be in jeopardy.
- The harasser owns the company, so there is no higher authority on site.
- The harassment has caused low self-esteem, which in turn creates reluctance to act assertively.
- The overall manager is a friend of the harasser.
- They fear they will be accused of being hysterical or over-stressed if they complain.
- They think it may go away if they ignore it.
- They feel somehow to blame for the situation.
- They are frightened the punishment may be out of proportion to the crime; they don't want to see the harasser lose their job.
- They are frightened of getting into the newspapers.

Taking the Initiative

Most large companies take the matter of harassment seriously, producing a policy statement and supplying guidelines as well as a set procedure for handling complaints. Staff should be made aware how they should go about seeking advice and what the formal procedures are, should the harassment be more serious.

The Industrial Society best practice guidelines state:

'Any responsible organisation should develop a culture in which sexual harassment is not tolerated. They must further ensure that any incidents which do take place are dealt with effectively, according to established procedures.

Guidelines on the handling of sexual harassment should be drawn up; managers and staff should be aware that sexual harassment will not be condoned or ignored. The effectiveness of the policy/ guidelines should be monitored.

The guidelines and the organisation's stance on sexual harassment should be clearly communicated to all staff.

Responsibility lies with senior management for formulating and publicising policy so that individuals understand what sexual harassment is and what they can do about it.

All managers should know that they have responsibility to step in and be confident about handling the situation.

Management training on the recognition and prevention of sexual harassment and on the implementation of the organisation's procedures should be provided.

Employees should be informed of their rights and responsibilities and know how to lodge complaints.

Totally confidential and sympathetic counselling should be available.

An independent, objective and appropriately trained individual or team of people should be responsible for investigating complaints according to procedural guidelines.

The nature and frequency of complaints received and the way in which complaints are handled should be constantly reviewed.

Sexual harassment should be covered by disciplinary and grievance guidelines.'

According to the Institute of Personnel and Development, investigation procedures should provide:

- Prompt, thorough and impartial response.
- Independent, skilled and objective investigators.
- Representation for both parties.
- Complaint details and the right to, and time to, respond.
- A timescale for problem resolution.
- Confidentiality for all.

Action Steps

- Decide what is and isn't negotiable and act to stop the unwanted behaviour as soon as possible. Hoping it will go away is unrealistic. It is harder to change a situation that has been occurring regularly for a long time.

- If the behaviour is inappropriate, don't collude in it by laughing or joining in, unless humour is appropriate (see below).
- Using humour may be an option. The well-timed one-liner can diffuse less serious situations.
- Avoid using overt anger or becoming visibly upset as this may place you at a disadvantage. You can tell the harasser how you feel about their behaviour but your comments will generally have more impact if they are spoken firmly and confidently.
- Be confident. You have the right to complain. Confident people rarely get picked on more than once.
- People can become aggressive if they are shown up in front of others. Unless the behaviour is seriously threatening it may be advisable to talk to the person in private.
- Never do this if you feel under any physical threat.
- Use positive body language when speaking to this person. Confidence can be shown by upright posture, positive eye contact and open, rather than closed, gestures.
- If the behaviour is serious keep a log.
- Get witnesses, if possible.
- Check out your company's complaints procedure.
- Ask what will be done about your complaint and what the timescale will be.
- Above all else, hold on to your self-esteem.

CHAPTER 8

Careless Talk

When I started at the company I learned pretty quickly that everyone there had a nickname. Then I discovered you were expected to keep the name they decided to give you. Some of them were quite funny but I felt mine was hurtful as it referred to my size. I'm embarrassed about being big but I tried to laugh it off at the time. Being called the same name every day wore me down, though. I couldn't ask them to stop now, if I did I'd probably get called worse.

Our boss used to come into the office each morning and call out 'Hello, girlies!' Some of the women used to laugh. They said that was just the way he was and that it meant he liked us.

Anonymous

Sexual harassment can take many forms, and not just physical. Much more common in business is the problem of what is and what is not appropriate verbal behaviour.

Swearing is dealt with in Chapter 5. Again, don't forget that we all have our own perceived levels of what is and isn't okay. But what about that good old British institution, the risqué joke? Should it be banned forever in the workplace? Is all the fun going to be removed from business by the PC police?

And what about teasing and name-calling? Aren't they just forms of affection? Should we go back to Victorian morals and cover our ankles and swoon at the first curse we hear?

Nicknames

The British are an emotionally stunted people, tending to use teasing as a sign of acceptance and comradeship. Hurtful nicknames are expected to be worn like a badge of pride. They start in the playground and never really go away. Hence Shrimpy, Chompy, Dumbo, Slap-head, Witless, etc. In a strange way, in some professions, the calling of names is a sign of bonding, as though you are being accepted into the group, despite your infirmities.

Refusing the nickname will be seen as a refusal to join in the gang. You may be accused of having no sense of humour, or being a killjoy. When the verbal insults are flying cheerfully it is difficult to stand up and yell 'Time!' without appearing stuck up and over-sensitive. This is a rite of passage and your response – in some business cultures – could be vital to acceptance.

So, what should that response be? Only you can decide whether the nickname is tenable. Some are obviously out, i.e. anything racist or overtly sexist. Does the title sound like a put-down? It could affect your standing in the company if it does.

In recent TV documentaries I have heard both Indira Ghandi and Margaret Thatcher described as 'girls' by contemporaries, and both were described like this when at the height of their power.

What do *you* feel the long-term effect is if a businesswoman is constantly referred to as a girl? The term even managed to place a rather frothy and lightweight spin on two of the most heavyweight women of our time.

Some sexist name-calling is more obviously untenable and should be strangled at birth. Interestingly enough, I can think of a whole list of female or gay put-downs, but only two heterosexual male ones. So men have a whole vocabulary of female-related put-downs to choose from, while women have a couple, neither of which have I ever heard a woman use in a work context, anyway.

Male-descriptive words are usually intended to be flattering. One of the biggest compliments a woman can be paid in business today is to be told she 'has balls'.

So, keep off the sexual put-downs and don't feel you have to tolerate them, either. And while we're about it let's get those pin-up shots off the walls as well.

It has long been known that women will not tolerate the sight of other scantily clad, pneumatic females adorning the walls of the workplace. It puts the female sex in their place as sex objects and demeans the working woman. Which is why the only pin-up shots I have seen hanging on office walls for the past decade or so have been of men! Evidently this is okay. Businessmen are obviously flattered by the sight of an alter-ego resplendent with baby-oiled pecs and well-padded pants. It shows there's more to men than meets the eye. Except it doesn't. If the pics of women have to come down, then so do the jock-shots too. Sorry.

Martian Chronicles

We all now know that men are from Mars and women from Venus but it is my theory that − in the workplace at least − even women can be Martians. The sex wars are alive and kicking in many offices, especially where women want to get their own back after years of supposed abuse.

In some business cultures even a mention of the word 'men!' can elicit a tutting and rolling of the eyes. To be fair, it is important that all sexist abuse is curbed, whichever way it rolls. Women slagging off men is no more funny than men slagging off women. We are all complex characters and generalisations are unfair, especially derogatory ones, even if you are joking. What is banned for men should also be banned for women. History doesn't matter. Mutual respect, please, it's the only way forward.

Own Goals

Some people manage to malign their own sex. I have heard women say that they 'would never work for a female boss' or that 'women just aren't good at making decisions in business', etc. There are women who think doors should still be opened for them by businessmen, and women who would never want to employ a female member of staff.

There are women and men who 'dumb down' for business, playing stupid as an act of manipulation. You know the sort of thing: baby talk, baby voices, flapping and fluttering and wide-eyed, feigned ignorance. Everyone has come across examples of grown-up female executives who get all pouty and coy when they want the fax machine mended, or intelligent businessmen who suddenly haven't the brain capacity to get a cup of tea from the machine or find out where the nearest dry cleaner's is.

Blatant Thoughtlessness

What about laddish behaviour or outbreaks of rampant girlishness? Is it correct for men or women in a mixed office to start boasting about sexual conquests? This has to be as demeaning as the pin-up pics as it works against the sex of the person being described. Also it is tremendously boring, as most colleagues are quick-witted enough to realise you aren't telling the truth. Apart from the long-term married ones, that is, who are well known for believing all the lies they are told about the singleton's sex life, resulting in a deep state of depression as they feel they are missing out and start getting nostalgic for their own, largely legendary, misspent youth.

Loud discussions of sexual prowess may also be as offensive to colleagues as swearing. Never assume everyone is fascinated. Many may well be repelled or nauseated. Younger folk, in particular, would generally be happier not to be forced to hear the gory details of the sex lives of anyone over the age of thirty.

There is little kudos to be gained by this type of showing off. Realise that colleagues will be laughing or gagging behind your back and give it up. When you start acting in a discreet way, they will begin to be really impressed and assume you are at it like a rabbit!

Compliments of the Management

Is paying a compliment sexual harassment? The obvious answer is that it depends what it is you are complimenting! I'm all in favour of compliments but – as a litmus test – try working out how the same comment would sound if you addressed it to a member of the same sex.

References to body parts are probably a no-go zone, as is anything said in a drooling tone of voice. If you want to pay a 'safe' compliment then say something nice about the person's work and avoid personal references altogether.

THE TOP TEN REASONS OFFERED TO EXCUSE
SEXIST BEHAVIOUR AT WORK

● I'm too old to change my ways now.
● I'm just a friendly sort of person.
● I'm just a tactile sort of person.
● I don't mean anything by it.
● I was only joking.
● Nobody else minds.
● I thought you liked it.
● Don't worry about me, I'm past it.
● Don't tell me you're one of those militant feminists.
● I'm afraid I'm just from the old school and believe in treating women like ladies.

The New Jargon

Most jargon is claptrap. Some of it is quaintly sexist, like the elderly businessman asking a client whether they were going to 'get into bed together on this deal?' or the business guru who describes the stockmarket as 'behaving like a greedy, demanding bitch'.

Then, of course, there is the age-old tricky problem of using terms like Chair*man*, spokes*man*, Dear sir/madam, etc.

I suppose it all depends how far down the politically correct path you intend to dally. I would suggest the use of the word 'person' instead of 'man' and I consider myself reasonably level-headed. I tend to write to 'sir/madam', though I have a colleague who uses 'madam/sir' and I suppose she has a point.

CHAPTER 9

The Casting Couch

I've never so much as been offered the opportunity of a
casting couch situation. At one time I thought it was a
myth, that perhaps it was something very 1950s or 60s
that didn't exist today, but then several of my girlfriends
and even more of my male actor friends have said
they've been propositioned for roles.
Maybe it's because I look like a tough person that
nobody's ever tried it on with me. Or maybe they have
made suggestions and I just haven't noticed.

Actress

She made it very clear that she fancied me and hinted
that my career wouldn't exactly suffer if we got it
together.

PR employee

The casting couch, a long-standing euphemism for having sex to get
either work or promotion, was for years a regular feature of certain
professions, like acting, modelling and film work. In some ways it still
exists in these professions, which tend to be less regulated and monitored
than other careers. A young actor called Neil, who came from Wales to

London to attend a leading drama school, discovered his first problems at the school itself:

'One of the male tutors must have spent twenty years trawling plays to find speeches and scenes that included men taking their clothes off. If you refused you were treated as though you were stupid.'

Women had similar problems in different classes: 'One girl was told to do a scene topless. When she refused she was told there were plenty of others who would.'

Neil has had fewer problems finding film work:

'Casting directors tend to be middle-aged women. They often flirt but I haven't been pushed to the floor yet. We've all heard of actors and actresses who have slept their way to getting film parts but the success is usually assumed to be shallow and they have little or no credibility in the business.'

Does the casting couch crop up in less aesthetic professions? Generally, the larger the company the fewer the problems, as set systems and busy, well-staffed and open-plan offices tend to prevent employees winging their way to the top via the bedroom. Personnel departments tend to be professionally run with little or no scope for more creative employment methods.

The staff responsible for hiring and firing in larger firms have to be accountable for their decisions. Stories of HR managers running interviews stretched naked on a couch with a flower stuck in their navel demanding to be persuaded into employing the interviewee are thin on the ground.

Approaches tend to be subtle these days, as in the case of a young salesman applying for a job at a small computer parts company:

'I felt the first interview went well and was asked back for a second, which I took to be normal procedure. This was run by just one of the women who interviewed me in the first place. We got on well and I became less nervous and got quite chatty.

Three days later her secretary called and said she'd like to take me out to dinner to discuss the job. The meal was quite friendly. She said there'd be quite a lot of client lunches and she wanted to see how well I coped. Again, I could see that would be normal and fair. By the end of the evening we'd both had quite a lot to drink, though, and she ended up offering me a lift in her taxi. I said 'no' and I never heard from the company again.'

Some claim to thrive on the casting couch system, like this account executive with a marketing company:

'I slept with my boss to get promotion. He didn't really suggest it, I think it just somehow happened. I felt my career was important enough to take the risk and I'm not ashamed of my decision. A girlfriend I told said he was just using me but it never felt that way. I know it was me who was using him.'

Nepotism always smells bad in any company and sleeping your way to promotion – even if it is at all viable – is not a way to gain the respect of colleagues. The whiff of favouritism around the most innocent of relationships can be enough to make a career untenable, owing to ugly reactions from other members of staff.

Offering work for sexual favours is archaic and inexcusable behaviour. Demanding a trade-in from people who may be desperate for a job is ghastly, whichever way you look at it. Countering such behaviour is difficult because job applicants will often be too demoralised and impoverished by their unemployment to push their case. Bad experiences can receive a passive response because the interviewee feels just too low to take things further.

Keeping Off the Couch

If you think you hear the squeal of rusty castors as the casting couch is wheeled in your direction, what should you do?

For a start, avoid any compromising situations. Thousands of jobs get advertised in the papers every day. Does this one appear to offer too much for too little? Does it imply there is an opportunity to earn easy money? Avoid interviews that are held in the private rooms of hotels unless you are sure the company doing the interviewing is sound. If in doubt take a companion with you. Never attend an unsolicited interview in a private home.

It has been known for interviews to stretch to dinner but make sure you keep the booze intake down so that you are in full command of your good sense. Avoid taking up offers of lifts home as this is where the problems can arise. Book your own return cab before you go out, if necessary.

If you feel uncomfortable about any behaviour during the interview stage it may be better to give the job a miss altogether. However, you still have rights. Again, keep a log of any suggestive behaviour and, if you want to take things further, you could write to the organisation asking why you didn't get the job (if that is what happened) and explaining how you feel your rejection was down to the fact that you wouldn't play ball. If the organisation's explanations are unsatisfactory you could take legal advice.

CHAPTER **10**

Virtual Sex

When we got back to work after the Christmas break we found someone had photographed their private parts on the photocopier and left a copy on each woman's desk as a New Year's present. Some women laughed but I know others found it offensive. The boss was furious.

When we first got on the internet there was a big rush for all the porn stuff. Everyone thought it was a bit of a giggle for a while but then they all got bored and I think only the really sad cases still do it now. The rest of us are just too busy working, anyway.

Anonymous

Now that the dirty mag in the top drawer of the desk and the walls adorned with pin-up calendars are consigned to the bin of pre-PC corporate history new methods have emerged for staff to get their gleeful rocks off in the workplace.

IT Sleaze

High-tech porn or 'virtual sex' is no better than the old-fashioned stuff and surfing the internet in search of rude bits is really no better than trawling the top shelf at your local newsagent, yet for some reason it is often seen as being less sleazy. Move over the dirty raincoat brigade and make way for the grubby mouse-mat set, perhaps?

Desktop Publishing

The average office desk will supply at least two methods of accessing porn: the PC via the internet and the telephone via the 0898 numbers. Whereas surreptitious reading of dirty mags was rendered difficult owing to the onset of the open-plan office, where every man and his dog would swiftly become aware of the exact nature of the contents of the locked third drawer down, sitting staring at your screen or with the telephone clamped to one ear will appear to be an innocent enough pursuit. Colleagues may not look closely enough to spot the rather more glazed than usual eyes, or the subtle sickly quality of the contented smile.

Who could tell whether you were listening chastened to an irate client or receiving some sort of 'I'm waiting for you to ring me, big boy' message on the company telephone? And is anyone sufficiently interested in your PC screen to notice whether you're viewing explicit pin-ups or the latest Dow Jones figures?

Ways to Tell if Your Colleague is Porn-surfing

- He or she appears unusually keen to set to work.
- They become uncommonly focused on their PC screen, ignoring greetings from colleagues.
- They become apparently oblivious to the perils of repetitive strain injury, sitting happily still and mesmerised by their screen for at least three hours over the recommended limit.
- If anyone gets near their PC they will either switch the whole thing off or throw their entire body over the screen.
- They claim their work is highly confidential, even when you know for sure that it isn't.
- They smile at their screen.
- They let out small nasal snorts at irregular intervals.

- There will be sudden clusters of colleagues of the same sex, all gathering round to stare at the one screen.
- Their expression can only be described as 'leering' as they do so.
- These clusters will suddenly erupt into guffaws of choreographed laughter and, when asked, they will claim it was the sudden erratic behaviour of the Hang Seng that caused all the excitement.
- He or she will spend a lot of time on the telephone, but without speaking.
- You will wonder whether sighing and making the odd gurgling noise is the recommended response when dealing with a client over the phone.
- They will slam the phone down quickly when the manager walks by, and without a single word of farewell to the caller.
- They will start making suspicious-sounding enquiries as to whether the calls from the office get monitored at all.

Scorched Earth

How to deal with office porno-freaks? You can of course report them, but you may prefer a lighter touch to handle what is – in effect – the behaviour of a naughty, pre-pubescent, spotty teenager.

You could try talking to them, as long as you have the appropriate evidence. Be gentle with them, even though you don't feel they deserve it. Explain that sex is neither dirty nor disgusting, but that you would feel better if they could confine their exploration of it to out-of-business hours. Suggest they find a partner and even try it for real. Tell them their skin will probably clear up if they do!

If the sleaze-merchant is your boss do none of the above. Dealing with *that* situation will require less sarcasm and more subtlety and tact.

You still have a right to complain even if it is your boss, though. Are you *sure* they are doing what you think they are? Check facts first. Most assertiveness courses will suggest a three-layered approach to difficult communications:

1. Show an understanding of the other person's feelings.
2. State your own feelings.
3. Reach a compromise.

How can this work when PC porn-grazing is the subject up for discussion, though? Could you really approach your boss and say something like:

> 'Nigel/Annabelle, I understand your need to sate your rather dubious sexual appetites via the internet. I realise that someone with your looks and personality may find it difficult to find any real-life love interest.
> I must say, though, that I find this pursuit offensive and sleazy. The noise you make is a distraction.
> What say you only surf between the hours of 1 and 2pm, when I am on my lunch break, or any other time that I am away from my desk?'

Maybe you should just try a brief outline of your feelings on the subject (without apparent emotion showing through) and suggest the behaviour is stopped. Be firm but not stroppy the first time you discuss it. If the behaviour doesn't stop after that, however, you may need to take things further.

E-mail

Of course, if the rudeness encroaches on your own territory, if porn or crude jokes or comments are put onto your own screen by e-mail, or if the soundtrack of the PC porn is played out loud, you may feel even more inclined to take action.

Gauge for yourself – do you find this stuff screamingly funny? Does it demean women or men? Would you mind getting chatted up via e-mail? The medium itself has created a whole new potential for the virtual date. Is it any better getting chatted up or harassed via your work screen than it is face to face? Again, the answer has to be subjective. If the messages being sent are persistent and embarrassing there is no reason why this shouldn't be considered harassment.

Is there anything to recommend using e-mail for social purposes?

Sad or shy types may find it easier to tap onto a keyboard what they couldn't say in person. But then there could be the humiliation of hearing guffaws and gagging sounds from the recipient, and watching as the e-mail is read by every person in the office.

E-mail has created a whole new medium for the love-lorn and, for those with a poetic turn of phrase, it can be used to great effect. This is the new way of flirting. Years ago great romances were kept alive by letter but, thanks to the advent of the telephone, the use of the written word as a means of seduction had virtually died out. Charming that it should be revived now, then. Do remember that you are supposed to be at work to *work*, though. The odd torrid epistle between consenting adults is wonderful but your boss may not think so!

Duplications

Oh, and just one other method of high-tech office porn: the Photocopy Flasher. Little needs to be said on this subject. Everybody knows one. Several people *are* one. Placing delicate parts of your anatomy onto the photocopier for reproduction isn't clever but – sad to relate – it is still quite funny in a stupid kind of way. I feel I should warn you at this point that other colleagues may find this sort of stuff very offensive, so only share the joke with those you know will find it as rib-rentingly hilarious as you do.

Also, remember that what may have been done in a rash moment as a dare is pinned to the work's noticeboard for at least the following week. Is this okay by you? If not, make sure you keep the only copy.

CHAPTER 11

Taking a Stand – How to Say No

We used to joke and flirt with one another – I think a lot
of staff do in our place – I just didn't notice when he
started being serious. It's hard to work out the right
time to say 'no'. When I did he just said he'd only been
joking and became quite offended.

Working overtime is part of the culture in our business. I
was never sure whether he was stringing the work out
longer just to ensure we were alone together or not. He
didn't actually make a pass when we were alone but I felt
uncomfortable sometimes, anyway.

Anonymous

The consenting stuff is part of business lore, then. Romances grow in
the office environment. Inter-colleague marriages are forged, earth is
moved and bums are photocopied. You may not have the right to join
in some of this behaviour at work, but you surely have the right to refuse
to. The only trouble is, then, how to say 'no'?

The word 'no' is one of the most difficult in the English language.
We may have been brought up to be passive. Refusing requests was
considered rude. Say 'yes' and please the person who asked. Say 'no' and
upset or anger them.

No Problem!

Business today is a whole heap of 'yesses', with work overload becoming rife and the phrase 'No problem!' on everyone's lips as a motto for good customer care. Companies have a 'can do' culture and negativity is unwelcome.

All this may be commendable as business practice, but it makes the act of saying 'no' at work even more difficult.

The Assertive Response

Being assertive means standing up for your own rights but without abusing the rights of others. It isn't win–win because the word 'winning' implies conflict. It entails both parties feeling good after a negotiation.

It is easy to see how this can apply to normal business transactions, where you are 'not refusing the person, only refusing the request'. When you say 'no' to sexual harassment or unwanted personal interest, though, you *are* refusing the person.

People rarely master the skill of turning down a pass or request for a date. Hence the age-old problem of 'being stood up'. Liaisons in private life can be littered with no-shows or no-phones when one party either bottles out of the date at the last minute or fails to phone when they said they would.

How often does the cry go up: 'Why didn't they just tell me they weren't interested? Why keep me hanging on like that? Why ask me out and then not turn up? Why say you are going to ring when you obviously have no intention of calling?'

Saying It Straight

Part, if not all, of the problem is the matter of communication. On the whole, people would rather be desperately rude and hateful than eloquent and honest.

Why all the hand-wringing when the truth is blatantly obvious? They did sort of want to go out with you but then they couldn't be bothered. They didn't ring because they didn't want to see you again. Did you really want honesty, though? At least with a no-show there is all the vicarious excitement of imagining your date has been locked in a lift shaft or eaten by aliens. Would it really be so good to be told to your face that they're very sorry but they really don't care if they never see you again? That one date was more than enough, thank you? That they'd rather stick needles in their eyes than have another one of those lengthy phone chats with you?

Business Wisdom

Standing a work colleague up is a much more complex matter, though, because you will be seeing their stricken little face the very next weekday morning and feeling their baleful stares on the back of your head as you go about your work.

Business colleagues are special and so are the relationships forged between them. You are a team working for the same goal (hopefully). Rifts are not always avoidable under the best of circumstances and it is always preferable to maintain the *status quo.*

Complaints about inappropriate behaviour can also backfire if they are not dealt with professionally. Not all managers can manage, and horror stories abound of bias seeping upwards as well as downwards, like this tale from a personnel officer in a major distribution company:

'A female member of staff went to a works party and was nearly raped by a couple of the guys there. She said events went from playful to scary. A union official found out and reported the incident to management, but he was just told to keep his mouth shut. I filed a confidential report about the incident but – to my horror – discovered it had somehow been circulated and read by nearly all the men in the office.'

Much of the onus for dealing with harassment lies in the hands of the company. Staff need to be trained in spotting incidents and in dealing with any that are reported. Procedures need to be specific and understood by all managers. Nobody should ever be busking it or playing things by ear.

As Railtrack state in their *Guidance Notes for Managers:*

'Managers and supervisors carry special responsibility by virtue of their authority over others. They may recognise that harassment, victimisation or bullying is taking place or have this brought to their attention, in which case they have a responsibility to ensure that swift and appropriate action is taken.'

The Measured Response

As noted previously, there are several ways of dealing with inappropriate behaviour. If you decide on a personal response, though, it is important that the message you send out is *congruent*, i.e. you appear to mean what you say. Often people will say one thing but give the impression the response is negotiable when in fact it is not. We may also appear to collude in inappropriate behaviour because we are embarrassed or indecisive about our choice of response.

Being congruent is not the same as evoking damnation and hellfire in an instant just because a colleague happens to compliment you on your new hairstyle. I am all for values but against overreaction and chips on shoulders. Before you decide to respond, ask yourself the following questions:

1. What is the overall impression that I want to give of myself in this situation? Do I want to appear hysterical and paranoid or calm and confident?
2. How can I best achieve that approach?
3. How bad is this behaviour?
4. Do I feel physically threatened?
5. What is my objective in raising this issue? Do I just want to see the perpetrator stopped or do I want to see them punished as well?
6. Does the punishment I have planned fit the seriousness of the crime or am I being guided by anger and a desire for revenge?

Once you have planned your ideal emotional response, start to plan how to behave within those guidelines. If you want to appear calm and confident then visualise yourself acting out those qualities. Anger and vengeance – however well deserved – will often alienate other people, while calm confidence rarely does.

I am not of the belief that some people are ready-made victims, either through behaviour or appearance. Bullies make their own victims and anyone can be singled out. I have met many people who have been bullied at work and the one thing I found was that they had virtually nothing in common, apart from their plight. Some had been assertive, a few even aggressive, and obviously many had been passive before the bully picked them out. If they all had a big arrow on their heads saying 'I am a victim, please bully me' then I couldn't see it, and a large part of my job is reading non-verbal signals that people send out via their body language.

Communication

If you are going to handle this situation yourself then you are going to have to have a stab at clear, concise, effective communication. Your message must be heard and understood. Hints should not be dropped. Sentences must be constructed. Rehearse, if necessary. Plan your response and hear it through your own ears.

Ask yourself, is your communication:

1. To the point?
2. Easily understood?
3. Too apologetic?
4. Too aggressive?
5. Full of irrelevant comment?
6. Specific or non-specific?
7. Tactful but firm?

So:

- Waffle must go. Practise until your speech is free of 'um, er, you know, sort of' etc.
- Fillet your talk. Pull out the backbone by analysing exactly what your main point is to be.
- Use the person's name to attract their attention.
- Book a time to talk to them to show how seriously you take the matter (but not if you feel threatened by them).
- Rid your speech of any irrelevant emotional content. When we decide to complain about someone we often feel like throwing in all the old gripes we can think of. Your point should be simple. This is not the time to air old grievances.

- Avoid emotional trigger words, like stupid, creep, slime-ball, hateful, and any other insults.
- Don't issue threats. If the behaviour persists you can tell the individual concerned you will take the matter further but don't go into your first meeting with all guns blazing.
- Back your message up with appropriate body language.

CALM, CONFIDENT BODY SIGNALS

Eye contact (shows you mean what you say)	Hands to sides or open gestures
	Sitting into the back of a chair
Upright posture	Serious facial expression

SIGNALS BETRAYING NERVES

Fiddling	Straightening tie
Looking down or away	Clearing throat
Smiling too much	Frequent blinking
Rocking leg	Running hands through hair
Foot-tapping	Breathless, high-pitched voice
Closed, barrier gestures, e.g. folded arms	Speaking too quickly, without pause
Perching on edge of seat	Not listening to other's words, too keen to get own message across
Clutching papers or bag	
Hands shoved into pockets	

SIGNALS BETRAYING IRRITATION OR ANGER

Clenched teeth	Jaw muscle working away
Hands into fists	Sighing
Clicking pen	Chopping gestures with hand
Tapping	Fiddling with change in pocket
Red face	Frowning
Staring	

SIGNALS BETRAYING TOO MUCH EMOTION

Crying	Not sitting still on chair
Shouting	Blushing
Pacing room	Hands to face
Wringing hands	Fiddling with hankie
Leaning over desk	Slamming door
Flapping hands	Swearing or any name-calling
Stammering	

Explain your emotions, but don't illustrate them. Do not sound ashamed of your message and do not apologise. Listen to the individual's explanation or excuses and understand what they are saying.

Effective Listening

To make yourself listen during what will be a difficult communication, you could try the technique of REFLECTING. This shows the speaker you have heard their point and avoids confrontation while forcing you to understand what they are saying. Reflecting is also a useful way of making another person prove their own point wrong!

To use the technique you should employ the full set of listening skills while the other person is speaking. Use:

● Eye contact.
● Nodding to signal understanding (but not necessarily agreement).
● Silence.

Once you have made your point allow them to make theirs. Listen in silence and don't interrupt, no matter how much you may disagree with what is being said. If they make a point and you jump in in disagreement you will end up in an argument. Nobody wins arguments because nobody backs down. If the other person is your boss you are especially unlikely to win any argument.

The technique is quite simple from then onwards. Once they have stated their case you summarise their main points if they have been wordy, or repeat their statement back to them if they have been brief.

It is important you get the inflection right as you do this. Never start by saying: 'So what you're trying to say is ...' You could try: 'So what you're saying/the point you're making is ...' or you could just repeat their words verbatim, but with a slight rise in tone at the end of the statement to turn it into a question, as in: 'You didn't mean anything by your actions when you patted me on the bum?'

This is largely non-judgemental but in asking for clarification you make the speaker explain further, which can in itself be a powerful tactic.

Never underestimate the power of silence. You should make your own point confidently and clearly, but after that be prepared to use pauses to illustrate calm and reasoned listening. If your objective is to get the behaviour stopped then this could be your best tactic. If you just want to vent your anger and appear irrational and hysterical in the process then go ahead and blow your top.

Controlled anger can be extremely effective, though. I mentioned in a previous chapter that you can discuss your emotions without displaying them and there is something far more chilling about someone who says they are very angry, but uses a calm tone of voice, than someone who rants *ad hoc*.

Saying Your Piece

Once you have planned and rehearsed your opening gambit and played around with the technique of reflection, you might like to second-guess the other person's arguments. Are they likely to agree and apologise? Might they deny everything and accuse you of being paranoid? Could they get angry? It isn't possible to predict accurately in what may be a stressful situation but you should prepare yourself for all eventualities.

Apology

This may seem like the perfect solution, and in a way it is. You may shake hands after the meeting and walk away friends. Was it all a little too easy, though? Keep your wits about you in the aftermath of such a meeting. Perhaps the apology was sincere but keep in mind that it is possible that it wasn't. If your career seems to slip into a gradual decline for no apparent reason following the meeting you may need to take the matter much more seriously. Start to keep a record of any unwarranted criticisms or negative reports. Ditto any instances when you were not offered any opportunities for promotion. Don't become paranoid, but do stay on your guard.

If a genuine apology is offered and accepted it is important you both return to normal working relations as soon as possible. Don't rush about telling colleagues you have 'won'. Never retell the whole incident with exaggerated claims of their humiliation and your own triumph. Be discreet. If stories of your boasting get back to the individual concerned they may undo all that you achieved so far.

The Right Turn of Phrase

When you decide to make your feelings known make sure you use the right words. Avoid anything too emotive or aggressive. Don't exaggerate, but don't understate the situation either. There is no need for you to apologise so avoid excessive use of the word 'sorry'. You are explaining how you feel and what you would like done about the situation. To get the message across clearly and effectively be tactful but to the point. Don't dilute it any more than you have to. Say the behaviour makes you feel uncomfortable and that you believe it is inappropriate. Say that you would like it to stop. If you feel it would help you could start by showing an acknowledgement of the other person's feelings, as in 'I know you don't mean to be offensive when you use that term' or 'I'm sure that nickname you call me is supposed to be funny but ...'

Going in with all guns blazing is an unwise option. If you need to know why you should tone down your reaction just remember:

1. You will have to work with, or possibly *for*, this person in future (if you aren't doing so already) and it is important to salvage the relationship when possible.
2. Most people respond better to reasoned argument. Aggression may escalate the behaviour.
3. You will create the best impression of yourself which will be advantageous to your career. Nobody likes working with someone who is known to go off the rails over what some may see as a minor

indiscretion. You may be dealing with a style of behaviour that your other work colleagues approve of or consider the norm. Taking a stand alone under these circumstances is an uncomfortable if unavoidable procedure. You need to get your point made and yet you probably need to remain on good terms with all involved, even if you dislike these people. This is another reason why the rational approach is the best one.

The Herd Mentality

What if you are the victim of more than one person? Bullies don't always operate alone. Sometimes a victim will find themselves being picked on by several of their colleagues. Teasing, name-calling or even groping may take place on a regular and widespread basis. This sort of behaviour may be part of the culture of the company, especially when one sex heavily outnumbers the other. Again, it is up to you to decide what you do or do not want to happen. Is the behaviour negotiable or do you wish it to stop? If you do then you are going to have to speak up or leave the company altogether. As with individual harassment, it is best to tackle group harassment as soon as it arises, rather than letting it go on, which may be seen as approval or collusion.

It is also best to mention it without employing visible emotions like anger. If you feel you can make a joke of it and still get your point across, then go ahead. If not, you will need to tell the group about your feelings on the matter while the maximum number are present.

If the behaviour is severe you will, of course, need to think about taking things higher. Speak to Personnel and find out who such complaints need to be lodged with. Before you do so, keep notes, as you may well be asked questions about the following:

● What exactly happened.
● Who was involved.
● When did it happen.
● The timescale of events.
● Whether you told the person/people involved to stop.
● Whether anyone saw the event/s take place.
● How often it has happened.

Legal Procedures

If you wish to take the matter to an industrial tribunal or court you are protected under The Sex Discrimination Act 1975. In the Industrial Society survey of 1993, it was found that:

'Of those harassees who filed a complaint or grievance, or who took their case to an industrial tribunal, 78 per cent and 70 per cent respectively reported an improvement. Although this suggests that strong official action is the most effective way of tackling harassment, the results show that only a small number (5 per cent) of harassees follow this route – perhaps because they are afraid of being seen as trouble-makers, or because they feel they will receive inadequate advice, support or backing for their case.

Under the Sex Discrimination and Equal Pay (Remedies) Regulations 1993, there is no upper limit on the award. Compensation is available for injured feelings and the award carries interest.'

The Manager's Role

The role of managers is a vital one in matters of sexual harassment. They should act as role models as well as ensuring no harassment exists between their staff.

At the building company Balfour Beatty, for example, they recommend that their managers and supervisors ensure that they:

● Maintain appropriate standards of behaviour from themselves and other employees.
● Recognise and deal with harassment by others.
● Stop racist/sexist language, jokes, abuse or victimisation.

CHAPTER 12

Lighting the Fuse

Everybody lets their hair down at the Christmas party. We've all worked bloody hard through the year and the booze is supplied free by the company as a thank-you, so it would be criminal not to take advantage of it.

Getting drunk is what they're all about, isn't it?

We usually behave ourselves until the boss leaves at around eleven and then everyone lets rip.

Anonymous

There are, of course, moments in the working calendar that can only be described as high-risk when it comes to sexual behaviour.

Most of these flashpoints include copious quantities of booze and a general mood of 'letting your hair down'. Alcohol may not be a sure-fire aphrodisiac but it's still the best excuse for uninhibited behaviour. Why spend days trying to pluck up the courage to tell Nigel from Accounts that you worship the ground his little Wallace and Gromit hand-knit socks walk upon when a couple of bottles of Blue Nun at the Christmas bash will have you ripping the same socks off with your teeth without so much as a hint of your previous diffidence?

The Office Party

These can vary between grim little Twiglet-and-lukewarm-fizzy-wine affairs, where everyone hovers wearing polite fixed grins while the parting Head of Office Supplies bores for Britain during their retirement speech, to vast drink-and-dance orgies where everyone gets down to the business of serious partying and inhibitions are left at the door with the coats.

The 'nibbles and stultifying speeches' dos are the least exciting and – obviously – least dangerous to attend. Watching someone unwrap a carriage clock or baby potty does about as much to raise the sexual libido as a trip to the dentist. Very little in the way of hanky-panky generally occurs at these events unless the punch is spiked.

The recipe for real sexual shenanigans must include any or all of the following:

1. Unlimited free alcohol.
2. Dim lights, so that even your more unsavoury colleagues might get momentarily confused with a sex god.
3. An opportunity to dress up and display flesh.
4. Physical contact encouraged via dancing.

Hands up, then, for the Christmas office party, that annual invitation to make merry and jettison your career in the process.

Christmas parties shine out like a beacon in most corporate calendars as the highspot of the year. 'Work hard, play hard' is still the adage in many companies, and much of the focus for the latter seems to be upon this event.

Now that the recession is over, many companies are lavish with their investment in this event and inventive in their selection of venue. Zoos, TV studio sets and museums are all popular choices and the refreshments available tend to be every bit as generous.

Whatever the scale of your company's beano, though, apply a note of caution before you turn up. Ask yourself:

● Do I like my job?
● Am I happy with my company?
● Am I ambitious?
● Am I in line for promotion?

If you answered 'yes' to all four questions then have a stab at the next, and probably most important:

● Will getting drunk and making an ass of myself in front of the boss really enhance my career prospects?

If the answer is a resounding 'no!' then read on. Staff attending office parties will often labour under faulty logic, believing the following to be givens:

1. The Christmas party is an 'off the record' event, anything goes and all is forgiven.

WRONG. No work-based event is *ever* 'off the record'. Behaving like a prat will always be memorable, far outlasting all those other highlights of your career, like the day you pulled in the biggest account for the company, or any instances of outrageous brown-nosing, like the time you washed and polished the boss's car.

Bad behaviour is bad behaviour and if it is visible, as it will be here, it will go onto some kind of a mental record. Groping or other unsolicited and noxious sexual stuff will be as off-limits here as it is anywhere else. The company still has a duty to ensure staff are hassle-free and so, therefore, have you.

2. If the boss behaves badly, then so can the staff.

WRONG. Bosses should be role models for other members of staff but unfortunately that is not always the case. If your boss is behaving badly you should in no way see this as *carte blanche* to do the same. Remember that the boss can't see how ghastly they are appearing, but they can observe you. Think about life at work during the rest of the year. Are you always allowed to do exactly what the boss does? I doubt it. Treat this event in much the same light.

3. Seeing the boss behave badly will only enhance career prospects as they will be frightened staff might tell their partner.

WRONG. Do I really need to explain this one? Blackmail was never a good career move. If they know you know things you shouldn't, they will want you out of the company. That is never a happy position to be in, in any organisation.

4. If the company is laying on free booze staff should guzzle as much as possible to get their money's worth out of them.

WRONG. Like sex, getting glassy-eyed on the odd glass of falling-down water is glorious fun, but – like sex too – it is generally better done outside the work environment. There's nothing wrong with getting a wee bit tiddly if you can handle the stuff with the appropriate amount of dignity but, unfortunately, judgement is often impaired by the mood of the moment; what was intended to be an inhibition-loosener often ends up becoming a rolling-under-the-table-clad-in-a-vomit-flecked-shirt kind of fiasco-inducer.

It is never wise to get drunk at any work event. Apart from the unintended sex that can occur, it may also bring on lethal bouts of 'finally telling the boss what I think of them' or even 'making a pass at the boss's partner without realising who they were'.

5. The Christmas party is an ideal time to get off with the colleague that you fancy.

WRONG. It may be the worst time if not planned with care. Always be graceful in your behaviour. Sexual harassment principles apply as much at this event as on any day in the working calendar. Nothing is off-limits. Go for it if you want to but don't be pushy if your colleague doesn't seem too keen. Never get fuelled up on Dutch courage first.

One phenomenon of the business party is that you may find yourself chatting up a colleague you don't even fancy. This is very much in the 'drink what I can because it's free' culture, and should never be encouraged. Using the bash as an opportunity to chat up a colleague you have always had your eye on is one thing but going on a binge is another.

And it doesn't always end with the chat-up, either. If conditions are right and cupboards available it is quite possible to cement the union *in situ*. This is, of course, a recipe for complete disaster. Perhaps the least career-enhancing incident on record occurred when one poor chap who had just started with a large and very prestigious marketing company found himself being seduced on the spot by a stunning stranger at the firm's party. It was only the following day that he discovered the woman was the wife of the managing director who had recently discovered her husband was having an affair and had gone to the bash hell-bent on revenge!

6. It doesn't matter what staff do at the party because everyone will be too drunk to remember.

WRONG. Some people drink and forget. Others – and the reasons for this have never been medically documented to my knowledge, though I am the living proof – remember everything in minutest gory detail, however out of it they appear at the time. I know several people with this uncanny knack and most of them are bosses.

Golden Rules

A few rules should be observed at any company get-together where the hair is likely to be let down:

1. Plan your ideal alcohol intake and stick to it. Water drinks down if you want to be seen to be making jolly along with those who have a strategy to get roaring drunk.
2. Have fun. Please. Nobody likes a party-pooper.
3. Only chat up people you know you fancied before the event. Lighting can play strange tricks. What you saw as a bit of harmless fun may have been taken a lot more seriously by your flattered colleague.
4. Never get too playful. The sexual harassment laws are a constant spectre at any business banquet.
5. Drunkenness will not be seen as an excuse or loophole for inappropriate behaviour.
6. Avoid having sex-on-the-spot. A quick snog under the mistletoe between consenting adults is one thing. It has even been known for the boss to go around brandishing the offending piece of foliage in an attempt at endearingly puckish behaviour. This should never be seen as the green light for Bacchic merrymaking, though. Remember:

- You could be discovered.
- You could get videoed by security cameras.
- You could get herpes or worse. Casual sex? Medical implications? Need I go on?
- You could ruin a perfectly good work relationship.
- You could look like a prat.
- Your reputation could suffer. Even in this day and age of sexual enlightenment people do have a tendency to turn a bit prudish

when the dust has settled. You may hear the word 'easy' or 'loose' applied to yourself in office gossip sessions, whether you are male or female.

The Client Party

It is difficult to imagine sexual goings-on at a client party without calling for a brown paper bag to ward off a panic attack. The words 'client' and 'making a pass' should never be mentioned in the same breath.

Don't.

Don't even think about it. It will all end in tears, and that's if you are lucky.

Parties hosted by or for clients should be libido-free zones. You are there to drum up work and create a good image on behalf of yourself and your company. There is no need to hit on a client to do that. Professionalism must be the order of the day.

Having said this, you may as well be told about the dubious client parties. Dodgy dealing is not unknown. Parties for clients can be arranged where escorts are booked as part of the deal. This may sound like something out of the Sixties, but, unfortunately, the tradition is still alive in some corporate cultures. How they choreograph these events without falling foul of the changes in business climate is beyond me. Would they be certain of the client's sex/sexual preferences? Do they ask before they book? Are male escorts provided as well? Researching this book has been fun but even I have my limits. Use your imagination.

Training Courses

In-house courses are rarely the venue for carnal behaviour but the same cannot be said of the 'on location' variety. Hotels are booked. Nights together are spent. Green lights are shown and free-for-alls ensue.

If any partners are thumbing happily through this book may I add here and now that this is not always the case.

Honestly.

Coupling on courses is the exception rather than the norm, but it does go on. You train together all day, you go back to the hotel in the evening. You eat together and get drunk in the bar later. You discover your rooms are on the same floor. A lot more has been started over a lot less.

It's true that training that takes place in hotels can give colleagues a valuable opportunity to bond outside the workplace. This is fine, and often one of the most useful by-products of the whole event. Socialising is useful because traditional business barriers and rivalries can be broken down.

Just make sure the same rules of sexual behaviour apply here as in the workplace, that's all. People like to sleep safe and hassle-free in their beds at nights.

Married members of staff can become particularly feral at such events as they consider themselves 'off the leash' for the night. This is tacky in the extreme. Stick a photo of your family on the bedside table and go and have a cold shower instead.

Part of the supposed fun can be to engineer bookings on a course to find an excuse to get away with the object of your devotion and get off with them. This is hardly taking a page from the Mr Darcy school of seduction, but it is nevertheless a popular and well-tried ploy.

Another phenomenon is the illicit colleague-couple whose existence seems to be one huge merry-go-round of training courses, booked purely so that they can continue their little off-piste affair away from prying eyes in the office. These are always married people who have spotted the untapped potential of carrying on an affair in cosy, warm hotel rooms that are paid for by the company. They are always spottable for three reasons:

1. Their names always pop up together for the same courses.
2. The subjects they train in are usually totally incompatible with their jobs.
3. They return to the company knowing precisely nothing about the subject they have supposedly spent three days training in.

Surviving the Survival Course

Many companies now elect to send their staff on countryside-based survival courses. These are seen as an exercise in bonding and leadership skills, but just how far does the bonding go?

As opposed to the hotel-based training course, where soft warm beds and alcohol are provided, survival courses usually entail a certain amount of 'roughing it'. For some this can be a passion enhancer but for most the prospect of wading waist-deep through an icy, mud-filled lake is enough to put them off sex for life.

Only the ruddy-faced outdoors types would call swinging from ropes an aphrodisiac, but there is something to be said for the heady excitement of achieving a physical challenge. Heroics can be a turn-on and so can all that fresh air. Things tend to get a bit back to basics and I suppose sex is about as basic as you can get.

Then there is the added problem of keeping warm during nights spent with just a sheet of canvas for cover. Stories will abound at some point regarding the concept of huddling together to stay alive. Just remember that this idea of huddling usually involves the whole party and not just you and the MD from Sales. Also, the whole idea of warming up is instantly negated if neither of you is wearing clothes at the time!

If you feel the need to indulge in a little 'huddling' while out on the moors just think twice about the colleague you find so attractive. Did you ever fancy them back at work?

Strange heroes emerge on these courses and you should understand that your judgement may be severely flawed. Just because the man/woman from Dispatch happens to hew canoes out of logs of wood with their bare hands is no real reason why you should throw yourself at their feet. Admiration for these skills is transitory. There is little call for them back in the workplace. You may be embarrassed by your choice once you return.

After-hours Seduction

Who can resist the lure of overtime? And yet this is exactly how the Don Giovanni school of line managers like to pave the trail of seduction.

For the truly *louche* this is the routine:

1. Bribery
   The object of desire is offered financial reward for staying late.
2. Lighting
   For some reason the office lights seem to have dimmed after six o'clock. Often the only light still working will be the desk lamp, with its sultry glow.

3. Disorientation
   Working late alone is an odd experience. The office is quiet. Body language and attitudes change. Ties get loosened. Things become less formal. You are hungry. You lose your sense of normality.
4. The Shared Elevator
   An excuse to break down spatial barriers.
5. The Meal
   Offered as a thank-you for work done, of course.
6. The Car
   It's too late for public transport once the dinner is over, so ...

Again, such behaviour is an abuse of power. This set-up is the work of the seasoned seducer. Watch it. Do your work, make your excuses and leave. Unless you fancy this person, that is.

What to do if a Client makes a Pass

In the world of toe-curling moments of pure, unadulterated, frozen-with-indecision embarrassment this one has to come pretty near the top of the heap. You may have been taught that the customer is always right but this is one situation where they definitely are not.

Fancying the client is very little help. Perhaps you are flattered by their interest and would like to reciprocate. Where will things end, though? What if you fall out? The ramifications could be ghastly. What you are going to need, whatever your final decision, is TACT.

Of course, the situation must be judged by degrees. If the customer has arm-wrestled you onto their desktop and has their tongue in your ear, tact may not be sufficient protection. No customer has the right to place their tongue into your ear unless your profession is of the type where events like that have been negotiated and paid for in advance!

Physical threats demand instant and possibly extreme action:

1. Say 'no' firmly and keep repeating it if necessary.
2. Yell for your mother.
3. Yell for anyone, a waiter if it's during a business lunch or a passing secretary if you're in the office.
4. Yell for more professional help, such as the police, if things are really out of hand.

Do you tend to flirt to get business?

Are you in the sort of job where you may end up alone with a client?

If you answered 'yes' to both of these questions I suggest you do less of the former and try to avoid the latter.

What about something a little less serious, like the common or garden pass? What if the client is merely trying to hit on you? How should you react then? This is a bit of an etiquette nightmare, but not an impossible situation. Ask yourself:

1. Does he or she know anything about your private life?
   Do they know whether you are already in a relationship? If not, then this could be your perfect excuse. Tell them you're flattered but spoken for. If you want to be really smarmy you could even try a few words of regret (but I wouldn't recommend it).
2. Can the pass be merely ignored as though it never happened?
   If the message was tentative it could be possible to parry it without being too blatant.
3. Were you groped?

If the pass was physical you may need to be a whole lot more articulate. For instance, there is no need for you to conduct a business lunch while a hand is on your knee or thigh. If you can, move yourself out of reach and say nothing, just carry on as though nothing has happened. If they still persist you will know you're in the company of a serial groper, which is a lot more serious than the one-off chancer.

Look towards the area of grope and say: 'I'm sorry, is my foot/leg/knee in your way?' If they are thick-skinned enough to say 'no' and continue you could try: 'Ah, so you're making a pass, then. Sorry, but I'm afraid I'm spoken for.'

Client gropes and passes should be reported to a manager as quickly as possible. Clients can be funny people and it has been known for the spurned variety to ring a company to complain about the member of staff who turned their advances down. These petty acts of revenge can be harmful so it's best for your side of the story to be heard first.

Some companies have more potential problems than others. The hotel trade, for instance, is generally well aware of the situation and most hotels give their staff advice.

'We have to ensure our staff feel safe here, under the Health and Safety Act', one leading hotel personnel manager told me. 'We take any problems very seriously, telling our staff to report any incidents. If the guest is a regular client we may get the guest relations manager to chat with them over a cup of coffee. If they are not regular it is probable they will not be allowed back. Often the duty manager will approach the guest and tell them they have upset the employee.'

CONCLUSION

So, sex in the workplace can be fun but it can also be dangerous. Perhaps that's exactly what makes it so exciting and tempting. You may meet your soulmate at work but you may also meet crisis if the affair goes wrong or signals are misread.

Banning sex from the workplace would be impossible. People spend so many hours there that consequently they have less leisure time, which means less time to search for a partner using more legitimate routes. Besides, proximity means you have time to get to know this person before you take the plunge and ask them out, which is a much less risky business than chatting up a stranger in a wine bar or club.

For some people the path to romance at work is smooth and trouble-free. Their eyes meet across a crowded desk, they date, they fall in love and they marry, still keeping their jobs and the respect and affection of their colleagues. Everyone is pleased for them and they are pleased for themselves.

Optional endings are possible, though, and this book has presented you with a few to consider before making your move.

Then there is the problem of unwanted advances. Laws had to be drawn up to protect those who cannot help themselves. You may be lucky. You might not have encountered rampant harassment or been a victim of it. It's easy to laugh at someone who does complain, claiming they should have handled the matter themselves, or that a swift put-down would have been enough.

We all like to think we can handle difficult situations with confidence, but few of us know for sure how we would react until we are put on the spot. Harassment is bullying and no one who has never been badly bullied should ever criticise the actions of those who have.

Then there are the work seducers who are almost comical in their efforts. Dressed appropriately, they'd be wearing a cravat and smoking jacket because that's the era where their techniques belong. Never be surprised at the lengths the true seducer will go to to catch their prey. Some will plan with extraordinary precision. I met one guy who arranged a whole morning of mock interviews in a leading hotel function room just so that he could pretend to offer me a contract for work and – guess what? – the paperwork just happened to have been left in his room.

Believing no one would go to such lengths I went into the room with him, only to hear the door being locked behind me. How did I get out of it? I'm tall and fit and he wasn't. The first punch knocked his dentures out! Someone smaller may have been less lucky.

The best way to cope with inappropriate behaviour is to:

1. Be aware.
2. Deal with the problem as early as possible.
3. Adapt your approach to suit the circumstances. Avoid overreaction but remember any threat of physical danger is best dealt with by a higher authority.
4. Keep a record if the behaviour persists.
5. Try to get witnesses if necessary. Keep in mind, though, that these witnesses may be less reliable if the harasser is the boss.

And if you're considering having an office affair yourself?

1. Avoid sneaky manoeuvres. Your relationships with your colleagues should be built on trust and comfort. Dropping hints or making subtle passes will destroy this situation.
2. Make sure there are no existing relationships on either side. Never believe anyone who claims their marriage is dead, but who is not divorced/separated.
3. Keep your career in mind. Things may not go well and the relationship might not be trouble-free. How will this affect your job? Few relationships end amicably. Visualise the situation before it occurs.

4. If you are a manager, think long and hard before starting a relationship with an employee. The employee may be under no obligation to agree to go out with you but are you sure they will know this? If the affair matures what will the employee's colleagues feel about the situation? Might there be accusations of favouritism? Will the employee be made to feel isolated among their colleagues? What might the long-term ramifications be? Does your company approve of relationships at work?

Just like any other aspect of your job, planning is vital, even – or perhaps especially – in affairs of the heart or loins.

See into the future. Plan for each and any possible ending to the affair. Keep things above board and make sure the other person isn't compromised at all.

Passion is wonderful, but so is promotion. If in doubt, keep your sex and work life separate.